MW00778850

VISIT

Loved Ones

IN

HEAVEN

Cover Design by
bespokebookcovers.com

Copyright © 2015 F.U.N. Inc.
All rights reserved.
ISBN: 978-0-9962166-2-3

VISIT

Loved Ones

IN

HEAVEN

Del Hall and Del Hall IV

Nature Awareness School

Manifest Your Divine Nature

UPLIFT
WITH DREAMS

F.U.N. Inc.

Acknowledgments

It is with the deepest love and gratitude we thank all those who contributed to this book. Their willingness to share some of their sacred experiences made this book possible. We hope their testimonies will inspire you with the possibility of visiting loved ones in Heaven.

The authors would also like to thank all those who helped in the editing of this book. Emily and Anthony Allred, Catherine and David Hughes, and Kate Hall. Your keen eyes and thoughtful suggestions made a huge difference in the telling of these heart-warming stories.

"The days of any religion or path coming between me and my children are coming to an end" saith the Lord

December 29, 2013

Table of Contents

Foreword

As the Earth spins along its journey through space and time, there is always an ever-shifting horizon where the evening gives way to the night. There, where a golden sunset retreats, parents in some land are tucking their children in for the night, perhaps whispering, "I love you; sweet dreams." As the stars appear, two lovers drift asleep in each others' arms, an old man shares words of wisdom with his son, a young woman whispers a prayer as her cat looks on from the foot of her bed, and a little boy curls up with his puppy.

On the other side of the world, the rising sun of a fresh dawn melts away the night, and dreamers awake. Some make notes in a sacred journal about their adventures in dreams, before those memories slip away like the stars of morning. Some start their day with a prayer, listening for guidance in that moment of stillness that separates last night's dreams from the pressing demands of the new day.

No matter what land we live in, what language we speak, or what religion has flavored our relationship with God, we all must sleep, we all have someone we love, and we all dream. Will you remember and learn from your dreams or will they disappear? We have found that this mainly depends upon the choices we make. In these pages you will find some dreams and other sacred experiences with the Divine which the writers made an effort to recall, and from which great blessings poured forth, and may now pour into your life as well.

Each of the writers you will find herein comes from a different background in life and has a unique relationship with the Divine. But there are a few things we all have in common. We all have a deep love for God, an unrelenting thirst for truth, years of persistent devotion to learning more about God, and our own place in the fabric of creation. Also, we have all spent many beautiful hours in prayer, study, and play at the Nature Awareness School, located on the edge of the wilderness in the Blue Ridge Mountains of Virginia. There, while studying in a simple classroom, sharing our joys over a hearty meal, dreaming in hand-made shelters, hiking trails to breathtaking views, or enjoying the refreshing waters of the spring-fed pond in the heart of the school, we have learned and grown over the course of many years. Our teacher, Del Hall, has built his life by listening for and acting upon Divine guidance. He has not only shared much of the guidance which he received, but has helped us learn the art of listening to and understanding the language of the Divine. Without the ongoing guidance of a Divinely inspired teacher, few, if any of us would have been able to appreciate the beautiful insights we have been given. Divine guidance and insights which are given in dreams, and in all aspects of life, are part of your birthright and inheritance as Soul, a child of God, for such is the true nature of you and me.

Do you remember a dream that seemed so real that your memory of it is much the same as an event from your daily, waking life? If you have experienced such a dream there is a very simple explanation for why it seemed so very real. The reason is, it was truly real. Perhaps you or someone you know has experienced a vivid dream with a loved one. It is very common for us to have dreams with those we love, whether it be a parent, child, teacher, sibling, grandparent, or even a cherished animal such as a dog, horse, or cat. Sometimes the dream provides insight about your relationship with the other Soul and sometimes you may spend time dreaming with a loved one who has departed this Earth. It can be bittersweet to awaken from such a dream as the joy of being with that loved one meets our sadness of knowing that they are gone from our outer life. But take heart and know that the experience was not "just a dream," it was a very real experience. A rapidly growing number of people are realizing that each is not just someone who "has a Soul." You may discover that you *are* Soul, a divine spark of God. This is something we have learned from experience.

Soul is the part of us which has no need of rest. We discover that we are free to journey through the many mansions of God's house. Our journey continues seamlessly while the body sleeps and even beyond the seeming borders of death. We have found that dreams hold some keys to a more abundant life and are windows into Heaven itself.

In these pages you will find precious experiences with the Divine, true stories of how lives and relationships have been abundantly blessed through dreams. These meetings with family members, beloved friends, and even with Prophets of God have deeply blessed us. We pray they may now bless you as well. Now is the time to seek your own deeper connection with God. Take down the walls which separate you from the Divine and discover a deeper peace and joy which is available to you. What are your dreams? Look for them, write them down, consider them in prayer, and discover more of the rich life you are already leading. Know that you need not travel through life alone. There is always a Prophet of God available to assist you, in dreams or in your outer life. Enjoy these true stories from our journeys and begin your own journey towards the very heart of God.

Timothy C. Donley

Student at Nature Awareness School since 1993

Preface

God's love and grace can bless us in ways beyond what many know, believe, or have been taught is possible. As a Prophet of God one of the greatest opportunities I have is revealing the many ways God can bless His children. One of the most heartwarming blessings is when He allows loved ones that have been separated by death to spiritually meet again. For over twenty five years I have led spiritual retreats in the mountains of Virginia and during these retreats many students have been reunited with loved ones.

Within the pages of this book are thirty-seven testimonies written by students of the Nature Awareness School. Each story shared is of a personal meeting they experienced with a departed loved one. If these children of God can have such profound experiences, then so can you. As you read this book please pay special attention to what my students were doing prior to their sacred experiences. All of the authors sing HU, a love song to God, daily. They pay attention to both their night dreams and awake dreams. Each knows the "Language of the Divine." They each have a personal and loving relationship with God's Prophet of the times and they allow the Prophet to guide them spiritually into the Heavens. They all love and draw nigh, close, to God daily.

This book shares a variety of uplifting and heart warming testimonies. There are meetings with departed children, parents, aunts, uncles, grandparents, close friends, and even beloved pets. In every testimony shared in this book the author received a healing of the heart. This book is being written with the desire to help heal YOUR heart. You too can sing HU, learn to pay attention to and understand your God given dreams, and learn to draw nigh to God daily.

All of us at the Nature Awareness School involved in the making of this book wish YOU, the reader, to be blessed by these true experiences. Perhaps by reading our stories you will be more alert to your own sacred experiences. God wants to bless you as He has blessed us. He wants a personal and loving relationship with you as he has with us. Perhaps these testimonies can provide comfort and confidence that your loved ones exist and are OKAY, even if you never have your own personal experience with them. As the Prophet of God I am here for anyone who desires to know the Lord's Ways, the Lord's Path, and the Lord's Teachings.

Del Hall III

Introduction

Life on Earth is an interesting venture for sure. It is here that we experience the joys and pains of the physical world. Of these, the loss of a loved one is for many the hardest. It matters not if it is a family member, friend, neighbor, or even pet. Love is love and loss is loss. Even if our faith in God and confidence in Heaven is strong, it still hurts when someone we love is no longer in our immediate reality.

For those that are not sure of the afterlife or if there even is one, the loss of a loved one can be even more upsetting. What happens to them? Is Heaven real or is it "lights out" forever? Are they okay? Do they remember me? Do they still love me? Will I see them again? These questions can rob us of peace and happiness in our daily lives. Imagine how much sweeter it would be to know with confidence, that even though you miss them, your loved ones are alive and well spiritually and you will see them again. Even better yet, you do not have to wait until the end of this earthly life to do so. You can visit them now.

But how you may ask? Part of the answer is contained within the following truth. You do not "have" a Soul, you ARE Soul. You ARE Soul first – you "have" a body. You are an eternal spiritual being within a temporal physical embodiment. When your body comes to its end, the real you SOUL, will continue on. Once again - you do not *have* a Soul, you *are* Soul, and so are your loved ones. This seemingly simple shift in perspective is actually of monumental significance. When considered, or ultimately experienced for yourself, it can open doors to even greater heights of wisdom, love, and understanding. It is this truth that accounts for the very real opportunity to visit with loved ones who have passed on. You, as Soul, can travel into the Heavens and reconnect with your loved ones.

Even though their physical body is gone, your loved ones still exist spiritually. The love connection you share is still alive and well. As a gift of love, God and God's Prophet can arrange for you to visit them again. Whether the meeting comes through a nighttime dream, a conscious journey into the Heavens, or in another way, it is very possible! I have been blessed to hear and witness countless examples of the healing that occurs, myself included, when someone has the chance to reconnect with a loved one who has passed on.

What an amazing blessing! How marvelous it is to see a loved one again… to hear their voice, smell their favorite perfume, or to feel their embrace just as real as in the physical. What joy to have an opportunity to look into their eyes and tell them one more time you love them. Even more so if you never had the chance to do so before they passed. These very real experiences are opportunities that will help heal your heart.

The stories in this book are just a few of the examples of the profound blessings gained from reconnecting with loved ones. The authors share their testimonies in hopes of inspiring you with the reality that you too can visit with loved ones who have passed.

Del Hall IV

HU – A Love Song to God

All the authors who contributed to this book sing HU daily. Many of their amazing experiences are a direct result of tuning in and opening their hearts through this spiritual practice.

HU is an ancient name for God that can be sung quietly or aloud in prayer. HU has existed since the beginning of time in one form or another and is available to all regardless of religion. It is a pure way to express your love to God and give thanks for your blessings.

Singing HU (HUUUUUU pronounced hue) serves as a tuning fork with Spirit that brings you into greater harmony with the Divine. We recommend singing HU a few minutes each day. This can bring Love, Joy, Peace, and Clarity, or help you rise to a higher view of a situation when upset or fearful.

1

Motherly Love Just When I Needed It

A strong love connection has no limitations. It is above time and space and the end of physical life will not diminish this love. Even so, what a joyous reunion it is to see a loved one again, hear their words, and feel their embrace.

Our lives are a collection of moments. Experiences and memories weave together to create the fabric of who we have become in the present. Our loved ones: family members, friends, and even pets play a huge role in our journey through life. The moments when we lose our loved ones can be some of the darkest in our story, but they do not have to be. The loss of a loved one is not the end of your love story!

My mother, Patricia, passed away on Mother's Day in 1998. I was sixteen years old.

My mother had been a part of almost every moment, experience, and memory that made up the fabric of my life. The thought of having to carry on and create new memories without her seemed overwhelming. Thank God for God! I have come to know that we are all in God's hands and that my love connection with my mother transcends our physical separation because she is still alive and well as Soul.

Thanks to God and His Prophet my mother and I have been blessed to share moments in dreams, awake dreams, and guided spiritual travels throughout the years since she passed. The timing is always perfect and just when I need motherly love and encouragement. One of my favorite awake dream symbols is seeing a red cardinal. I started to notice that when I was thinking about her or missing her I would see the flash of a red cardinal. The cardinal would usually land on a branch directly in my view and then once I got the message fly away. To me the bird represents the love connection that my mother and I still have even though she is no longer with me in the physical. Every time I see a red cardinal it is not an awake dream, some are just birds, but I know in my heart when it is a message.

I was also blessed with a very special night dream sixteen years after her death. I am a mother now, with my own family and children. One day while driving in the car, my daughter asked me if she would ever meet my mother in her body as I had known her. I explained that her body was gone forever but that my daughter could meet her as Soul or in a new body if she reincarnated. That same night I had a dream where my mom (in the form of her physical body as I remember her most) was sitting on the edge of my bed. I walked into my bedroom and she stood up from the bed and hugged me. I could feel her body and smell her. It was the same hug I had known and missed for so many years. In the dream I was conscious that it was present day and that she should not really be there physically and how special it was to be seeing her.

She told me that she was proud of the woman that I had become and the life, family, career, and home that I had created. Hearing her voice again was music to my ears. I was in high school when she passed away so her words, expressing that she approved of the choices I had made, were more than any daughter could hope to hear. It was a REAL experience and interaction and a true blessing from God. I am so grateful for the opportunity to reconnect spiritually with my mother. I am also thankful for the wisdom I have gained to cherish every moment I have with other loved ones while we are still together in the physical.

Written by Catherine Hughes

2

Closure With Grandma

We live in a temporal world where everything has a beginning and an end. Soul however is eternal and carries on after it's time in the physical world; it does not cease. In the dream state you can visit with loved ones who have gone on before you. These encounters are not simply wishful thinking on the mind's part, they are real experiences and a profound blessing.

One night I had a dream with my grandmother. She had passed away some time ago and I had never been able to have that last conversation with her. I only got to say a quick goodbye on the phone the night she passed.

In this dream we got to spend some time together and have that conversation. I was getting out of a vehicle in a restaurant parking lot and I was looking around. This place was not familiar to me. I saw someone waving at me from the front door. It was my grandmother! She looked much younger than her years. She was smiling and waving me over. I ran to her and gave her a big hug. We walked in, sat down, and began to talk. We talked about all of the things that I had wanted to tell her before she passed. I had a chance to tell her how much I loved and missed her and thanked her for all she did for me in life.

I felt like the Divine set this up for the both of us. We both had things that we felt we needed to tell the other, and through the grace of God we had the chance to do so. I am so grateful to the Divine for allowing me the opportunity to spend that time with her. It meant so much to me to tell her, face to face, one last time that I loved her.

Written by Anthony Allred

3

My Dad Helped Me From Heaven

Dads can shower their children with love in many ways. It may come as a smile, or pat on the back, words of encouragement or wisdom, quality time together, or in the following example - a reminder to check the oil in the mower. The fact that the reminder came in a dream after the author's father had passed demonstrates how this love transcends physical life.

While growing up I loved my dad dearly. He was loving, gracious, and had a good nature. He taught my brother and I many outdoor sports such as skiing, ice-skating, canoeing, sailing, archery, and shooting at cans with his .22 rifle. We spent many hours enjoying the outdoors with him and my mom, camping and doing many of those things that he taught us. As a teenager I would help him in his carpentry business by painting and staining wood trim. I enjoyed hanging out with him in his workshop while I helped him with projects and we talked about all sorts of things. After my brother went off to college we bought season passes at a ski slope nearby and we spent many hours skiing together. I was his precious little girl and I always knew that he loved me. I thought that he would always be there for me.

I was seventeen years old when my dad was diagnosed with an inoperable brain tumor. The doctor told us that with radiation treatments he might live for another five years. Back then, in the 1970's, no one talked with the patient about how serious their condition was or that they might die. But somehow he knew. Because we didn't talk about it, we never got a chance to say goodbye. Two months after the diagnosis, even with the treatments, he was in the hospital dying, unable to communicate with us. During his time in the hospital he visited me in a dream. He was going up and down in an elevator. I saw him, though we didn't speak. Somehow I knew that it was real and we were really together.

A few days after he died I planned to mow the lawn. He had given me a nice new bright yellow lawn mower about a year before, after the old one quit working. He even put on a miniature license plate with my name on it. A loving touch. That night I had a very clear dream. He came to remind me to check the oil in the lawnmower. The next day before starting up the mower I remembered the dream, so I checked the oil. The oil compartment was bone dry! Thanks dad for your help in a dream! Back then I didn't know whom to thank for giving me the dream, but I was grateful for it.

Over twenty years later after getting married and having two children, I began going to the Nature Awareness School with my husband. I learned about the Prophet of the times and that he blesses us with dreams. One night I had a dream where I was told that I was now allowed to see my father. He appeared before me and I could see his facial features very clearly. He looked strong and healthy, like he was before he got sick. We hugged and hugged for a long time. He felt so real and so solid. It was so good to see him, to hug him, and to feel his love again. I felt such intense joy seeing him. I said that it had been twenty-two years since I last saw him. Gosh twenty-two years! When we stopped hugging, he disappeared. What a gift that was! It was real. We were two Souls seeing each other again after almost twenty-two years. Thank you, Prophet!

And now, for the rest of the story. Several years after that dream I learned, through many awake dreams and a knowingness, that he had reincarnated into another body as someone with which I have a very close relationship. God has blessed us with being together again. Our love continues, beyond death and into life again!

Written by Diane Kempf

4

Friend That Passed is Happy

When we pass on, our earthly possessions stay here but we hold onto the thing that matters most – Love. Our love connections carry on to the other side and we meet our loved ones again. Sometimes, even before we leave the physical we are blessed with a reunion.

I grew up with my childhood friend Lisa. We were six months and two days apart. On every birthday for as long as I can remember we exchanged phone calls on our special days. Lisa passed on a few years ago and when my birthday was coming up this past year I knew that I would miss her and her phone call.

I attended a 3 Day Spiritual Retreat at the Nature Awareness School before my birthday this past October. It was where I had a beautiful and real experience with Lisa that left me with much comfort and peace. We were both sitting on a huge boulder/rock which was up the street from where we grew up and where we had spent a lot of time hanging out as kids. The rock had ready made seats carved into it and I remember sitting there with her many times in our own seats with our feet dangling. It was the coolest spot and we had some of our best childhood times there.

In this gift experience we were there again but it was oh so different. Lisa was beautifully alive and happy. She was brightly lit and shone as herself, as Soul. The whole rock area was brightly lit up as well with soft golden light. My spiritual guide Del, the Prophet, was standing above us on the level part of the rock. He was with us as Lisa and I talked. We expressed things that we needed to share. After this I gained clarity and was able to be at peace with her death because I knew she was and is in God's Hands. She is happier than she ever was and is a bright and beautiful Soul that is alive and eternal. This was a huge gift and blessing given to me; an opportunity for me to heal, let go, and know on a deeper level that she is okay.

When my birthday rolled around I thought of Lisa, but I did not experience that sadness or cry those tears like I had the year before. After all, I had just seen and talked to her a few days prior.

I was happy in knowing that she is definitely happy too!

Written by Moira Cervone

5

A Prayer Answered

I have looked this testimony over many times while trying to create the best introduction possible for you, the valued reader. It is a touching story of the loss of a loved one and the author's journey through life afterwards. It contains wisdom on many aspects of the journey of Soul while here in the physical. What though is the pearl? Is it that "you are eternal," or maybe that "love transcends death," or perhaps that "you will see your loved ones again?" Maybe it is that "our prayers are heard." This testimony contains wisdom on all of the above but to me the true pearl is this; you can, in full consciousness, be taken into the higher heavens if you have a teacher who is authorized to do so. The Prophet is a teacher and guide of this magnitude. There is no limit to your growth and splendor as Soul if you have a teacher who can help you connect directly with the Divine. I have been witness to countless healings, miracles, and growth in consciousness through the years from the Prophet helping people do just this. What is keeping you from experiencing more joy and love? What is the prayer in your heart? Are you looking for someone who can help you grow spiritually? I know where many have found their answers.

Early one morning, when I was fifteen years old, my grandfather woke my brother and I up and sat us down on the sofa. My mother came into the room and she was crying. I was pretty sure she was going to tell us that my great grandmother had died. We had never had someone close to us die before. Instead, my mother told us that our father had unexpectedly passed away. It was a devastating moment in my life. It hurt so much that I closed down, withdrew, and put walls up around myself. For years I prayed to God, all I wanted was thirty seconds more with my father to tell him how much I loved him and to say goodbye.

I started searching for answers: Is there life after death? Where do we go when we die? Why are we here? Is there really a God? For many years I felt like my father was watching over my family and I, and that he was helping, protecting, and guiding me. I hoped this was true.

The death of my father affected all of my relationships. I always held something back, perhaps trying to protect myself from reliving that kind of pain again. Though, I softened some as years passed, I was never really all in; not with my mother, brother, wife, children, or friends. With the birth of my children my heart did begin to open more and the walls started to melt down.

Approximately twenty years after the death of my father, I had a very unexpected experience at the Nature Awareness School. During a guided spiritual journey my spiritual teacher Del, the Prophet, took me into the inner worlds – the heavens – in full consciousness. I left my physical body, and as Soul, traveled with my teacher and visited my father. My father was healthy and younger. He sparkled and glowed and looked like he was bathed in a soft white light. He was filled with such an incredible love, more than I had ever experienced from him in the physical. I got to tell him how much I love him and missed him, which he already knew. We flew together in the heavenly worlds and it was as if time did not exist. I will never forget this experience. When it was time to come back I really did not want to leave him. I did not want to lose him again. But one of the things I found upon returning consciously to my physical body was that my father and I have a love connection that will always be there. Before this experience I felt like I had a huge void or dark spot in my heart, now that was being replaced with love.

In one brief experience the pain that I had buried down deep inside was healed. From that moment on, everything in my life changed for the better. This healing (which is one of many experiences I have had at the Nature Awareness School) has effected my life in ways that have been so life altering and so positive that I do not have the words to express it in a few brief paragraphs. God's Divine Grace healed my heart and removed the walls around it, allowing me to give and receive more love in all areas of my life. I now enjoy more joy, true peace, abundance, and love than I could have ever imagined possible.

Written by Jason Levinson

6

Sending Love to My First Kitty

It is a gift of love from God when we are reunited spiritually with our loved ones and pets most certainly qualify! The comfort that comes from this blessing can heal the heart.

In September 1995 my family had to put my cat Tigger to sleep. This was very unexpected and I did not get to say good-bye to him before it happened. I missed him very much and wanted to see him again.

Even at an early age I knew how to sing HU, a love song to God. It had often brought me comfort. I decided to sing HU with the hope of seeing Tigger again. After awhile I felt my body relax and me, as Soul, spiritually leave my body. I then spiritually traveled to a beautiful meadow filled with wispy grasses and wildflowers. I knew Tigger was around, so I called out loud "Here

Kitty, Kitty, Kitty!" I used to do this in the physical to get him to come when we were outside together. Sure enough, Tigger came running towards me. Tigger was followed by a little girl who was wearing a purple dress with a floral print on it. I picked Tigger up and hugged him tight to me. He began to purr so very loudly and licked my face. I felt Tigger's very real love for me, even though he was no longer in a physical body.

I was eight years old when I spiritually traveled to visit my kitty. To this day many years later, I still remember the love and comfort I felt from that experience. At the time, the Prophet wasn't as much of an integral part of my life as he is now. But even so, I was blessed with the chance to see my beloved cat again and to say good-bye. I now know that the Prophet took me spiritually to see Tigger and that it was a gift of love from God.

Written by Michelle Kempf

7

My Grandparents Make My Heart Smile

The passing of a grandparent is the first real loss that many will experience in their lifetime. It is also one of the last understandings our grandparents help us to realize while still here in the physical - cherish your family because life is precious and life is short. Their first lesson to us from the other side - Soul carries on and there is a place for us in God's Mansion!

Growing up I was blessed with fabulous grandparents. I have such loving memories of our time together. Sadly, they have all passed from their physical bodies. God has blessed me with experiences with each of them to reassure me they are okay. When we leave this world we indeed continue on and we can still visit with our loved ones.

My mother's father was nearing the end of his life and I had the feeling I should fly out to visit him soon. Before the trip, I was blessed to have an experience with him during a retreat at the Nature Awareness School. I was singing HU and could see him in front of me; I was able to tell him how much I loved him. I expressed to him that I was praying we could see each other one more time. I also saw my grandmother during this experience and I let them know I was really grateful and blessed to have them as grandparents. I also told them I would miss them greatly when it was their time to continue their journey. I then saw my mother, who had passed years before; she was waiting for her father at the gates of heaven. This was my confirmation that there was not much time left and I was so grateful to God for giving me the nudge to go visit my grandfather one more time. My siblings and I made the trip across the country to visit our grandparents; it even worked out so our cousins and aunt could meet us there. It was such a wonderful trip; I have many fond memories of our time together. It was such a blessing to visit with my grandfather one more time before he passed.

Years later I had another experience with him, my grandmother, and my mother. While I was singing HU, I saw the three of them together again. My grandmother had just passed away and I saw my mother and my grandfather welcoming her to the next world. As my mother welcomed her father years before, together they now welcomed my grandmother. They were all so happy to be together again and to continue on their journeys as Soul.

My father's mother recently passed as well. Not long ago, I had a dream with her. In the dream I was at an ocean running down the beach. There was a huge wave coming to shore. My grandma was walking down the beach with a baby. They were walking hand in hand down the beach at the water's edge; I saw a large wave coming to shore. I was trying to get to the baby before the wave came upon shore, so the baby wouldn't get sucked under the water. I ran to them and picked up the newborn baby and hugged it. In the dream I wasn't worried about my grandma because I knew she was okay. I knew I needed to pick up the baby. The wave wasn't large and scary, everything was calm and peaceful. When I awoke from the dream I felt peace that my grandma was okay.

A few months later, during a HU sing I was brought back to this dream by the Prophet. While I sang HU I saw blue, white, and gold waves of light coming through the room and I felt as if I was at the ocean. I was transported back to the dream/experience with my grandma and the baby at the ocean. I was now standing on the beach with the baby and I saw my grandma floating out over the ocean water, she was very peaceful. My grandma floated over to us and went into the baby I was holding. I also felt my grandpa's presence; he passed many years before my grandma. He was very happy and peaceful as well. During this experience I knew they were both okay and that they were both continuing on their journeys.

I am so grateful to God and the Prophet for these experiences. I truly know when we leave our life here we continue on and can be reunited with our loved ones. It is such a blessing to know that we can connect with our loved ones, Soul to Soul, before and after they leave this world. I miss having my grandparents with me but I am comforted to know, without a doubt, that they are happy. When I think about my grandparents, my heart smiles.

Written by Emily Allred

8

Hiking With Mom in Heaven

It is a sacred opportunity and blessing to visit with a loved one who has passed away. Because we are personally known and loved by God, sometimes God will answer additional prayers of the heart during these reunions. In the following example the author had the chance to experience the trip he had wanted to take with his mother.

My mother passed away recently at age eighty-eight. She had a strong faith and often spoke joyfully about going to heaven when her time came. In fact, she specifically requested that my three brothers and I sing at her funeral the old hymn, "When We All Get to Heaven."

She had been widowed at age fifty-five when my father had a massive heart attack. She never remarried. She continued to teach elementary school for ten more years, then retired to enjoy a life of volunteer work and traveling. Upon returning from one of her trips to Ireland, she said she wished I could have been there to hike with her in the beautiful countryside. I wished I could have been there too!

The last few years I watched her body decline, but as Soul, she remained her delightful, joyful self. As she needed more and more help with daily living we spent more and more time together. The bond between us grew through many weeks of cancer treatments and hospitalizations. When she breathed her last breath, it was bittersweet. I know she is finally where she longed to be, and yet I miss her.

Soon after her passing I was blessed to be at the Nature Awareness School. A group of students and Del, the Prophet, were singing HU, a love song to God. During the silent time after singing, Del appeared spiritually in front of me on the inner and took me to see my mother! She was standing in a beautiful green meadow. The day was unusually bright and clear, with a hint of cool breeze. Mom's appearance was just as it was in her middle adult years, still with the natural color in her hair. She was wearing brightly colored clothes and sunglasses, with a big smile. She was so happy to see me and I was so happy to see her. She beckoned me with her arms to come walk with her. We hiked along together through the meadow and up a light brown dirt trail up into the surrounding hills. As we went higher we saw the beauty of the meadow from above. It was more beautiful than I could ever imagine Ireland to be. We spoke no words, sharing love and joy in our hearts to be hiking there together, fulfilling our wish from many years ago.

When my awareness returned to the room where I was sitting, I was glowing with love and gratitude for Del, the true Prophet, for taking me there. What an amazing gift! I now know for sure that mom really is happy and well and that she still loves me dearly.

My brothers and I look forward to singing joyfully at her memorial service, "When we all get to heaven, what a day of rejoicing that will be, When we all see Jesus, we'll sing and shout the victory!" I have no doubt she will be singing with us!

Written by Paul Sandman

9

Dreams Have Kept Our Relationship Alive

Even though our time in the physical comes to an end, we will see our loved ones again. Until then, dreams afford us with a very real opportunity to continue our relationship by spending time together. The love we experience in dreams is just as real as in waking life.

My grandmother passed away when I was a young child. At the time I was confused about her death and it was the first time I can remember experiencing the feeling of loss and deep sadness. We were very close and I loved her very much. Sometime shortly after her death I had a dream with her. In the dream we spent time together in her workshop. She used to make beautiful stained-glass artwork and windows. I sat on her workbench and watched her make stained-glass windows, enjoying our time together. I do not recall us talking in the dream but I experienced the bond of love we shared. This dream brought me a lot of comfort during a time of hurt. My heart began to heal from the loss and over the years I would have a dream with her from time to time.

I had dreams where she was at some of my sports games cheering me on. I saw her seated in the bleachers smiling and happy. These dreams were so real that when I would wake up a part of me knew that she was not gone forever and she was fine wherever she was. At the age of twenty I moved from a small town in Colorado to the Northern Virginia area. This was a big transition for me. Shortly after my move I had another dream with my grandma where she looked at me and into my eyes and said, "It's all alright." I awoke from that dream with a feeling of comfort and peace that I cherished during a time where everything around me was new and unfamiliar. My dreams had become a way for our relationship to continue even though she had passed on.

A few years after my move, I began taking classes at the Nature Awareness School. There I learned that dreams are a way that the Divine communicates with us and each of us has our own personal dream language. This resonated with me and my dream experiences over the years with my grandmother only confirmed this truth. The School helped me really claim that these are REAL experiences. This realization has been a beautiful blessing in my life and it's shown me that our loved ones live on beyond the physical. The dreams with my grandma over the years have brought me comfort, love, peace, and helped heal the hurt I experienced in her passing.

Our dreams are REAL experiences. We may not always understand them and sometimes they may seem convoluted. But I can truly say that I understand more of my personal dream language through the spiritual tools I've learned at the Nature Awareness School.

Written by Shanna Bixenmann

10

Gifts of Love and Healing

What a blessing to be able to tell your father you love him one more time before he passes. Especially when you recognized and followed God's guidance telling you to visit him "NOW." An even greater blessing – learning more about giving and receiving love and being granted yet another chance in a dream. This time being able to more fully exchange your love.

Several months before my dad passed away the whole family helped my mom make the tough decision to place him in a health care facility. His cancer was rapidly progressing. My mom had made the attempt to care for my dad at home, but he required more and more involved and specialized care. This was taking a huge toll on my mother both physically and emotionally. My mother no longer drove, so I would pick her up once or twice a week to take her to visit with dad. Each time we visited we saw dad becoming weaker and weaker from the cancer.

One cold morning in early March my mom informed me she was not visiting dad because she was not feeling well. My first thought was to stay and visit with her and visit my dad later that week when my mom would be feeling better. However, I received a very powerful "nudge" from the Prophet to go see my dad NOW! I definitely followed that nudge! As I entered dad's room at the health care facility, I saw immediately that he was very weak. He had difficulty talking, so I sat close to his bed and held his hand. It was such a gift to just sit and hold his hand. As I was leaving I leaned over and gave him a kiss on his cheek and said "I love you dad." He replied back to me in a whisper "I love you too." That is the last time I saw my dad. He passed away quietly the next day.

I am so grateful to the Prophet for the blessing of that "nudge" to visit my dad and to be given the opportunity to tell my dad I loved him. Sadly, love was something that was not expressed or demonstrated much in our household when I was growing up. Being able to tell my dad I loved him and hearing that he loved me was a huge gift. Over these past years since my dad passed away, the Prophet continues to bless me with his love, guidance, protection, and truth. One huge truth his guiding love has shown me is that I was not open to love. I did not know how to express or demonstrate love to my loved ones. Hearing and accepting this truth has literally saved and changed my life. I am forever grateful for the Prophet's gift of waking me up to love.

In February of this year I was blessed by the Prophet with a beautiful dream about my dad. In this dream I was at my mother and father's house, the house where I grew up. I was in the kitchen. My dad was sitting at the little kitchen table drinking a cup of tea. When I walked into the kitchen he stood up to greet me. He was young! His hair was dark not grey and it was cut in a crew cut style of his younger years; a style I vaguely remember from my childhood. He was very relaxed and peaceful. I walked over and gave him a big hug and said "I love you dad." As my dad hugged me back he whispered in my right ear, "I love you too." I know that dream was a real experience.

The Prophet knows me so well and loves me so much that he blessed me with the dream experience that was absolutely perfect for me. He knew and understood how important and healing it was for me to tell my dad I love him now, after learning more about love. I felt that I could actually send love from my heart better now that I had learned how to accept love. Before I learned how to accept love I could not really send love genuinely to loved ones. I thank the Prophet for this amazing, healing, and life changing experience.

The memory of this dream gives me a glimpse into the full spiritual life that I and each one of us leads beyond our day to day physical existence. It is a memory of a real life experience that I think about often and genuinely cherish.

Written by Donna Hospodar

11

Cathy's Black Lab

*What a gift to see a loved one again after they have
passed on from the physical. It matters not if human or
animal because love is love. Either way it is a joyous
reunion and special blessing.*

For about thirteen years I had a pet black
Labrador Retriever named Callie. I adopted her
when she was six weeks old, and she was with
me until she passed in 1998 of declining health
and old age. I have no children so she really was
almost like a daughter to me. I loved her dearly
and felt very sad for a long time after she died.

I am blessed to have had several dreams
about her. In one of the dreams she was a
puppy, and I was taking her for a ride in a basket
that was attached to the handlebars of the
bicycle I was riding. She was happy and healthy,
and we were having so much fun together! In the
dream I could feel the wind blowing on me as I
rode the bicycle. I could also feel the love I have

for her and the love she has for me. It was a beautiful experience. I had a dream about Callie this year, many long years since she passed. In this dream she was a little older. We were having a happy, playful, loving time together. I was petting her and she was dancing around me, wagging her tail in delight.

These dreams, these gifts of love from the Divine, warmed my heart and brought back fond memories of our time together. The dreams are such a blessing to me. I know these dreams are real! Animals are Soul, too. The dreams about Callie reassured me that she is still alive and happy in the other worlds. The love we have for our loved ones, including our pets, and the love they have for us lives on after they have passed. I am deeply grateful to the Divine, and my spiritual teacher, the Prophet, for these beautiful personal gifts of love.

Written by Cathy Sandman

12

I Saw Neale Again

When your time here in the physical world comes to an end you will carry on in the other worlds of God - it is not "lights out" forever. Believing in life after death is one thing. It is quite another to know this truth from personal experience.

For several years I had been attending classes at the Nature Awareness School and was blessed with my own experiences of Heaven. I had experienced this many times and knew that Heaven was real and that loved ones were truly in a better place after they died. I knew they would be okay and that they were still loved by God. This all became even more real to me in April 2005. It was then a high school friend of mine was in a severe car accident while driving home from work. He was alive but in shock when first responders arrived on the scene. He was taken to a local trauma hospital where he was pronounced dead.

When my dad told me that Neale had died, I was in shock and disbelief, even as I saw the tears in my dad's eyes. As details of Neale's accident and medevac flight came out, it became more real and slowly sunk in. I was very upset and disturbed by it all. I felt a strong urge that I needed to see my teacher at the Nature Awareness School. Fortunately that same weekend there was a spiritual retreat scheduled.

I attended the weekend retreat and on the last day of class, just hours before leaving, we did a spiritual exercise as a group. While singing HU, I saw Neale walk into the room with my teacher, the Prophet. Neale gave me a big hug and I knew that he was okay. He looked happier and more alive than he ever did on earth. I got to see firsthand that after a loved one translates to the other side, whether they believe in God or not, they spiritually live on. This experience has brought me so much peace in the years since Neale's passing. I know without a doubt that there is indeed a place for all Souls in God's mansion.

Written by Michelle Kempf

13

Visit to Grandma's House

In this wonderful touching story about a visit to "Grandma's House" the author's grandmother is still alive but separated by distance and the desire to move on to the heavenly fields. This experience afforded her the opportunity to visit spiritually and shower love on her grandmother before she moved on.

When I think of her the first thing I see is her smile with a long bright row of straight beautiful teeth. She speaks her mind and lets the chips fall. She loves baseball, card games, and romance novels. She is a caretaker. At forty-six she had the last of five children. Give her a cigarette, a cinnamon bun, a cup of coffee, and she is in Heaven.

This wonderful woman is my grandma. At eighty-nine years old she has always weathered illness and bounced right back. Recently she was not feeling well and was talking about moving on from this life. She has been dreaming of fields of orchids. I have seen these fields too while visiting the Heavenly Worlds and I am certain that God is preparing her for the next adventure. She lives in another state twelve hours away, but on March 15, 2015 the Prophet read my heart and I found myself standing in the center of her familiar kitchen while my body sat here in Virginia. I was attending a class at the Nature Awareness School and we had just finished singing HU. My heart was filled with love. I sat in the quiet time afterwards listening for communication from God. My awareness drifted to my grandmother and in an instant the Prophet took me to her. I had many experiences at once, like a movie playing out, but better because I was not just seeing. I was there in the present time and also re-living some of my most fond visits with my grandma.

The first thing I saw was her coffee pot and I could taste the salty coffee. We had a lot of laughs about this over the years. She had to soften her country water with salt. Then I saw the cookie jar that was almost always filled with homemade cookies. I felt my hand run along the orange counter tops. I could feel the wind blowing over the cornfields and through the screen door in the dining room. I smelled the light scent of manure from the farm down the road. I felt the quiet openness of the property and in the living room I saw my grandpa watching westerns in his recliner.

I felt my face pressed against the brown shag carpet as a teenager on a particularity long holiday visit. Then I was a child again staying up late playing cards with grandma as she smoked cigarettes and told stories. I saw her making homemade noodles and a piece of ravioli being tossed into boiling water. Then I saw her sitting at the kitchen table. The Prophet stood behind her smiling. I cupped her face in my hands and said, "I love you, Grandma." Then I was clapping for her. "Bravo!" I kept repeating. My heart swelled as I congratulated my grandma on a life well lived.

It means everything to know that my grandma is in the care of the Prophet and that while her body is going through a rough time she is perfectly fine. I also got to love on her and appreciate all the beautiful ways she has touched my life. This was so much more than remembering. God allowed me to re-live these precious moments in time. Sometimes the "little things" that make up my daily life seem like they will happen forever, but nothing stays the same for long. These moments once passed become the "good times" of life.

Thank you, God, for reading my heart and taking me to see my grandma once again. Thank you for giving me peace to know that she is in your loving care. When I call her she is confused and does not want to talk for long. It means so much that we were able to communicate Soul to Soul and I could tell her how I really feel before she passes.

Written by Carmen Snodgrass

14

Brother's Passing

Losing a loved one is hard enough. It can be even more challenging when they take their own life. Too often people fall into feeling guilty at what could have been done to prevent it. This is a losing battle, one that will close your heart and pull you down. We must accept that they are ultimately responsible for their decisions – the good ones and the bad ones. We must also have faith that God does indeed still love them and that they will not be eternally damned. Ask yourself if this is your idea of something a loving God would do, punish you forever for one mistake? Eternity is a long, long time. Would you cut off your child forever, withdrawing all love for one lapse in judgment? Are those that take their own life still loved by God – absolutely. Are they still held responsible – absolutely. And what does that look like? Most likely a quick return into a new body to begin again. Usually into a similar situation where they have another chance to face the challenges they struggled with before. Life is about growing into greater capacities of wisdom and love and it takes time. Time that a loving God graciously gives us.

October 21, 2008 I received a call from my mother who was frantically repeating over and over, "We lost him; we lost him." My oldest brother had died. He struggled most of his adult life with bi-polar episodes. Numerous bi-polar episodes and other serious ups and downs took a toll on his marriage. After a divorce his life became more unstable and by August, 2008 his life seemed to be spiraling downwards. On his birthday we talked by phone and I was looking forward to having time with him in person at Thanksgiving. That time never came.

After starting a new job in another city he became extremely depressed and ended up at the mental health unit. On that fateful day my parents had gone to petition for his early release into their care, saying that they could provide a safe environment for him. My dad had left the keys to the car by the phone, and when they were all napping, Dave got up and slipped out of the house. The car was his means to end his life.

My family was grief stricken and my parents were full of guilt. I also wondered what I could have done differently and I too started feeling guilt. In contemplation, connecting with the Prophet on the inner, I received very strong inner guidance not to allow my heart to fill with guilt.

He assured me that anything I might have done would not have changed the outcome for Dave. I felt a release from guilty feelings shortly after my contemplation. Without the guilt I was more able to support and comfort my family.

Two weeks after Dave had passed I prepared for my early morning contemplation, singing HU and connecting with the Divine on the inner. Instantly I found myself at a favorite spot by the pond at the Nature Awareness School. The Prophet was standing to my right and my attention was drawn to the left by some movement. There was my brother Dave, looking like he had in his late twenties. He looked robust and healthy. I was very happy to see him. I introduced him to the Prophet but then realized that Dave already knew the Prophet because He had brought Dave to me. My gratitude was immense to be with Dave once again.

My mother and father continued to suffer deeply with grief and guilt. I always thought my dad would live to be at least a hundred years old. He now seemed to age rapidly and was rather miserable and somewhat bitter. A month after his ninetieth birthday he had a stroke and died. I did not have the opportunity to say good-bye. Six months went by and one evening as I sat down to HU at bedtime, suddenly there was my dad! He looked much younger, glowing with good health. It struck me how happy he looked and totally at peace. I do not recall him looking that happy or peaceful, ever.

I am very grateful to the Divine for giving me these precious experiences with my brother and my dad. Both experiences helped to heal my heart from my loss. And even though my brother ended his own life, breaking spiritual law, I know God still loves him and will care for him.

Written by Jan Reid

15

Father Daughter Dance

God knows the prayers in our heart and can answer them in many ways. Many people miss these profound blessings because they are not tuned in to receive them. If we are conscious daily of God's presence anything is possible.

Ever since I was a very young girl I dreamed of my wedding day. I dreamed of finding someone to love and share my life with. Someone to enjoy being with each day, in the big and little things of life. I imagined my dad walking me down the aisle and dancing a father and daughter dance. Well, I found the man of my dreams and we are getting married in a few days. However, it seemed the father and daughter dance could never happen. Two years ago my papilino (what I called my dad) passed away. I have really missed him and am very sad he will miss my wedding. Having my dad at the wedding was a big part of my childhood dreams.

The other day my fiancée and I had a date to go to an art show. The artist is a dear friend of ours. My fiancée came down with a really bad cold and could not attend the event. I decided to stay home with him, but he insisted very much on me going. I am so glad I did go! I had a great time seeing friends and amazing artwork. Little did I know the surprise God had planned for me.

One of my friends got engaged earlier that day and as she was sharing I was given a Divine spiritual travel experience while standing there listening. It was like I had a dream while awake, but it was a real experience. My spiritual teacher, the Prophet, took me spiritually as Soul, to the venue where my wedding was to take place. Music was playing and I found myself dancing the father and daughter dance with my spiritual teacher. What an amazing gift! As my heart filled with gratitude, I saw my dad, my dear papilino standing right next to us. He was there to dance with me! We danced! It was a beautiful moment that I'll cherish forever. He looked wonderful, healthy, happy, and could dance!

God knows me so well! He knew I missed my dad so much and orchestrated this tailor made experience for me. God gave me a gift that keeps on giving. I can sing HU and ask to relive this experience. When I relive it, I am there again, dancing with my father. I have learned to be aware of God's presence. While my friend was sharing about her engagement I had been aware of a Divine presence. I believe that awareness tuned me into Divine Spirit so I could receive this gift.

Being aware of God and His Prophet has changed my life drastically for the better. It is like I have a brand new pair of golden glasses on. These golden glasses help me see the Hand of God much more clearly in my life. I am so thankful to God for this gift experience with my dad.

Written by Olga Boucher

16

Visiting a Beloved Pomeranian

Losing a loved one is a hard enough without the additional worry of not knowing if they are OK on the other side. The following dream brought peace that a beloved pet and companion was more than just OK, but was doing extremely well.

It was a beautiful Saturday morning, the last day in May. The kind of day where you thank God to be alive and experiencing such a day with your loved ones. I was starting breakfast in the kitchen. I'd find out in a few minutes that my daughter and her fiancée were taking care of her chickens next door. Her little Pomeranian, Dallas, was with them, or so I thought. Actually he had bolted off and my daughter thought he ran over to see my husband and I, as he often would.

The front doorbell of our house rang. Who could be there at 7:30 AM on a Saturday? I went to the door, inviting my inner spiritual guide to come with me and bless whoever was there. Two men were there. One of them asked me, "Do you have a little dog? Looks like a Pomeranian?" "Yes, is he alright?" I replied. "He's dead. My truck hit him in the road" the man said.

It felt like the world turned upside down. My daughter loved Dallas so much. He'd been with her when she first went out on her own, was with her in college and nursing school, through her first job, and now living with her and her fiancée. He was a constant companion, a constant joy and comfort, adored as a family member, with a distinct beloved personality. I prayed with my spiritual guide the Prophet, and sang HU. As I looked towards the gate between our properties and wondered how in the world to tell my daughter, she came through the gate towards our house with a big smile on her face. She thought Dallas was with us. As I told her the news she wailed with grief and sorrow.

To say it wasn't easy would be an understatement. However, we felt very blessed that the men had stopped to come to our door. Otherwise we might not have known why Dallas was missing or found him much later, horribly, in a ditch by the road. My daughter never blamed herself or God for what happened, but said all things happen for a reason even if we don't know why. She was terribly upset that Dallas, wherever he was now, was scared and was wondering where his "mommy" was. That evening I prayed to our Heavenly Father asking if my daughter could be blessed with a dream that would comfort her in some way. Later, my daughter called me to express she was very worried that Dallas felt alone. I suggested she pray for a dream with him. The next morning she called me to say she hadn't had a dream about Dallas. She was still so worried about him. I explained it had only been one day since she prayed and to be patient, continue communicating with the Holy Spirit and that I was praying also.

Several mornings later she called to tell me she was given a dream, a vivid dream, more vivid than she could imagine. Dallas was well, more than well! I encouraged her to write her dream down while it was still fresh and vivid. Here are her words: "I was traveling in a car (possibly with my fiancée) to meet my mom. She was in a lush, beautiful garden. It was a public garden, reminded me of the national gardens in DC. Felt like there was a rotunda there. My mom was a school teacher and she had a group of young children with her. They were standing together in a group off to one side. The grass was very green. I got out of the car, saw my mom and the group of children. Everyone was very calm. Standing next to the children, in the grass, was Dallas. He looked the best I had ever seen him. His eyes were bright and sparkling. His fur was long, brushed out, and very, very shiny. There was bright glowing sunlight illuminating his body from behind him. His facial expression was calm and serene, yet he looked WISE - as if he knew something I didn't. He looked at me, and his eyes relaxed slightly. He just looked peaceful - like he did when he used to stand in the wind. I looked at my mom and said 'Is that Dallas?' the dream ended."

Through this dream my daughter found peace and healing. As we talked about the dream she realized God loves her. The Prophet was in the dream but since my daughter is so comfortable with me, her mom, she saw only me and not the Prophet who was with us. God had blessed her by pulling back the curtain and showing her Dallas was safe, comfortable, peaceful, and whole in one of God's Heavens. She was still sad and missed the little fellow, but she was able to move on in life and stay in balance, knowing that he was well. Sometimes our prayers aren't answered this quickly. Sometimes we forget our prayer and fail to understand when the prayer is answered. The Voice of God must have determined it was in my daughter's best spiritual interest to answer her prayer, and my prayer, quickly. Praying on behalf of others does have an impact. God listens to each prayer and responds in the way that is best, as only God knows, for each Soul.

As an epilogue, my daughter and her fiancée had planned to go away to a nice resort the very next weekend to celebrate her birthday. She wondered if they should go now. Maybe she would be so sad she would spoil the weekend for her fiancée and waste a lot of money. She prayed about this. They made a decision to not go to the fancy resort, but instead chose a town an hour and a half away so if she began to feel very sad, they could come back home and wouldn't be out a lot of money.

I received a phone call that weekend. My daughter was so excited because they had walked to an area that had an historic public garden, and it was the same garden she saw Dallas in during the dream, complete with a peaceful rotunda! She was so joyful to receive this final confirmation that Dallas was OK and that her dream was real. The Hand of God had guided her to this town, to this garden, to show her that Dallas was indeed well cared for in the Hands of God, and so was she. So are we all! It was a wonderful, joyful, and peaceful weekend filled with loving memories of the little fellow. My daughter was then able to begin a search for a Pomeranian puppy and by August she joyfully welcomed the new puppy into their home. Has anyone ever told you that God loves you? Did you hope it was true? It is!

Written by Martha Stinson

17

Forever Young

The hardships and loss we might experience while here on Earth can sometimes be our greatest teaching opportunities. They propel us to seek answers to life's questions or to draw closer to God for comfort and understanding. This growth in wisdom and love are ours to keep way beyond a single lifetime.

Over twenty years ago my "new best friend" Fran stepped up to the plate to be my maid of honor at my upcoming wedding. Fran was the kind of light filled Soul you just were drawn to and wanted to be around. She always had a positive outlook on life and shared everything with you. Her generosity and thoughtfulness of friendship and time was always so evident. She agreed without hesitation to be my maid of honor and said we would have fun together planning my wedding. I was so thrilled to have a friend like Fran; nothing deterred her from her loving task to assist me. About four months before my wedding Fran told me she was a breast cancer survivor and that she was presently in remission. It was no wonder she had such exuberance for life and thanked God all the time for this second chance at living it so fully.

Our plans together took shape over the months as we became close friends. I loved that she shared deep spiritual thoughts with me. We had discussions about her views concerning death. She told me she had taken care of her mother who died of cancer a few years earlier, and then ignored her own medical checkups after finding out she also had cancer.

It was two weeks before my wedding and I noticed Fran didn't have the liveliness and energy she used to have. Fran confided that her cancer had metastasized. True to form, she swore she would be fine for the wedding and nothing would come between this happy day and her! True to her word, it was amazing to see how well she kept everything organized and on track, helping me with every detail. Fran thrived when she didn't dwell on the medical concerns ahead of her. She looked absolutely radiant as my maid of honor and was so excited to wear a favorite dress that belonged to her mother.

Fran shared with me her many thoughts about life and what happens after we die. As her radiation and chemotherapy treatments progressed she said no matter what the outcome, she was fine as she had peace in her heart. She shared that her life had been worthwhile. She seemed to have an inner knowing that we are just passing through this life wearing these "earth suits," and the real world was where ever God is and she was going there. She had a very rare acceptance of death and never expressed any fear. I admired this beautiful quality about her and learned much during our short friendship.

Nine months after the wedding had passed, I went to visit Fran at her father's home. The treatments had stopped working and she was terminal. It was a beautiful May day and she asked me to take her outside in her wheelchair so she could feel the sun on her face and smell the freshness of spring. She was stunningly lovely and happy in this moment. She shared that she didn't think the end would come this soon. Eight days later she passed peacefully away at home. That beautiful Soul left her pain filled body to soar home to God.

As her illness progressed, Fran had planned her funeral as a happy remembrance of her time with all of us. She even had the countenance to have a significant song played for all of her friends at her funeral. It was called "Forever Young," and it carried a message for all of us to remember her by, and take to heart.

Some months had elapsed after Fran's passing. My route home from work took me past the cemetery where Fran was buried. I thought of her often when I came to this part of my drive. One day I was thinking of her with much love and gratitude for all the many things I had learned from her. Just as I came upon the cemetery the song "Forever Young" came on the radio! I was so overwhelmed with love I had to pull the car over as the tears flowed. The Divine had heard the prayers in my heart as the loving memories flooded so dearly through me. What a precious gift! I know now this was an awake dream, a daytime spiritual experience. I shared my experience with my husband and he exclaimed the same experience had happened to him as he drove by the cemetery! We expressed how grateful we both were at this extraordinary gift!

There are times I've asked my inner guide and spiritual teacher Del, a Prophet of God, if I can see Fran in a dream and I've had various nighttime dreams with her. We are just hanging out being friends. Fran always appeared much younger, quite lovely, and as vital as ever. In one particular dream she was helping me with a relationship that had ended painfully for me. In the dream I was sitting on a couch with several other people watching a television show. The person who ended the relationship was lying across our laps. He was very heavy and I told Fran how angry I was. She and the other people looked at me questionably. I was struggling to get out from under his weight all the while talking to Fran. During our talk her loving demeanor helped change my attitude from one of hurt and anger to happy, positive, and free from the negative emotions I was holding. I had become free from all those negative emotions. A heavy weight had been lifted from me. I miss Fran dearly to this day but will always be grateful to have shared this lifetime with her.

Written by Nancy Nelson

18

I Saw My Mom When She Was Six Years Old

The author of this story was blessed to travel back in time and experience a part of her mother's childhood. Wow! Other than the obvious, "that is way cool," three things really jump out to me. Dreams are real experiences in the greater worlds of God, love transcends time, and God reads the prayers of our heart. It is such a comfort to know this.

I was taking a trip to Long Island. It was going to be a quick trip, just up and back within twenty-four hours. My mom passed away sixteen years ago and had grown up on Long Island. I was only going to be there a few hours but it was really important for me to take the time to see some of her childhood. I really wanted to see the house she grew up in and also a bakery that she frequented as a child.

Two nights before I drove to New York I had a very real dream. It was one of those dreams where when you awake, for a moment you are not sure if it was a dream or if you were really there. I was really there. In the dream, I was with my siblings in New York trying to find the house my mom grew up in. As we were walking through the streets of New York, we passed through a wedding. The streets were filled with people in attendance. They were all singing HU, a love song to God, as part of the wedding ceremony. We enjoyed the wedding for a few moments and then continued on to find the bakery. As I walked in, I realized it was no longer there, it had been turned into a Starbucks. My mom came through the front door, she must have been six or seven years old. As she entered the scene slowed and began to transform back to how it would have appeared many years ago.

In this dream/experience, I was allowed to experience this part of her life with her. I was taken back in time and actually lived this moment with her. It was so very real, I could feel the shelves and cabinets, could smell the bakery, and could see and hear her childhood laughter and joy. When I woke up the next morning I was very emotional and still felt as though I was there. I could still feel the emotions that I felt as I lived this moment with her and I could still smell the bakery. It was such a real and wonderful experience.

When I arrived in New York I found the house she grew up in and then went to find the bakery. I was eating lunch in a restaurant on the street where the bakery was located. I asked the waitress where the bakery was so I could see it. She said it was no longer there. As I sat there and began to feel sad that I would not be able to see it, a girl walked in off the street with a Starbucks cup (there was a Starbucks across the street). I immediately was taken back to my experience in the bakery with my mother, right back to how I felt being there with her. What a wonderful gift the Divine had given me, I was allowed to actually live that moment with my mother when she was a young girl rather than just walking through a bakery fifty years later. This experience was such a gift to me and I am so grateful to God for this time with my mother. God knew it was in my heart to see a part of my mother's childhood. The Divine not only helped me see part of her childhood, it allowed me to experience it with her.

Written by Emily Allred

19

Our Beloved Daughter Rayne

Beyond the experiences in life that hurt deeply - there is more. Beyond the loss of our dearest loved ones - there is more. There is love, and gratitude, and beauty, and goodness, and a God who loves us. Life can be so much sweeter for those that have the eyes to see.

About sixteen years ago our daughter, who was twenty-seven, lay in bed at home. Her hospice nurse had been with us for several days and she had gone home to change clothes.

Rayne had been diagnosed with Hodgkin's disease when she was twenty-one. A lot had happened in those five and a half years; a lot of chemo, a bone marrow transplant, and almost total body radiation. But there was more. She got to go to Puerto Rico to visit her cousin Tania, who was more like a sister, and she got to ride on a jet ski in the ocean, and she got to fall back in love with the boy she had loved in high school. He was the one who she was with on the jet ski. But there was more. She got to see some of the really important stuff. There were many people who stepped up and went way beyond anything they had to do. There were incredible nurses and doctors, and a woman who worked in housekeeping, who did not speak English, but always said hi, and Rose in x-ray who always took time to talk to her, just to name a few.

Rayne said one time that given a choice, she would choose to go through it all again. To be sure some stuff was gone, but there was so much more given. There are many blessings, even in something like this.

For the past twelve hours or so she had been struggling to breathe, and her eyes were closed, and she had not responded to us in any way as far as we could tell. I had been lying next to her petting her face, and telling her it was OK, it was OK to go. I had heard her father outside in the night asking God to please take her. Rayne's effort to breathe was increasing, and as we prepared to give her more medicine, all of a sudden I was drawn to look at her face. Her eyes were wide open, her breathing peaceful, and her look was amazing! It looked like utter, complete, joy - like she saw everything, beyond what you even know to hope for, beyond this world.

After a moment, that also seemed to be forever, her eyes closed and she stopped breathing, and her heart stopped beating.

We got to see her, see. We got to know she's better now, with God. There's always more, because there's always God.

One time, not long after I had started going to the school, Del led us in a spiritual experience. I got to touch her face, and hear her voice.

I knew I missed her. I knew I would love to see her. But I did not know how much I longed to touch her, and hear her voice.

He did.
Thank God.

Written by Pam Kisner

20

Granddaughter's Wish is Answered in God's Time

*God answers a prayer of the heart by allowing two
Souls the ability to share time with each other in a way
that had not been possible during physical life. This
beautiful example of visiting a loved one in Heaven
shows once again that we are each loved and known
personally by the Divine.*

My grandmother Deni was a loving grandmother, but not the openly affectionate type. While I knew that she loved me and my siblings, there was an unspoken understanding that we were to remain on the quiet side and not disrupt the grown-up conversations. I remember hearing "hush sweetie" frequently, and relished in the moments when I got to share something with her without being overshadowed or over-spoken by others. One of my favorite memories with Deni involved being taken on a vacation with just her, my sister, brother, and grandfather and having their undivided attention during meals and around the pool as we relaxed and talked.

As the youngest, my older siblings reached the age of being able to stay at the table after a meal and talk with her, while I ran off to play. She was an educated and fascinating woman and loved to talk about books, art, or current events. Topics well above my childish talk of bugs and soccer. Yet, she passed on before I reached the age of being able to relate to her as an adult. However, the Divine had not forgotten this wish, or prayer, in a granddaughter's heart to be able ` to talk and speak heart to heart with her grandmother.

As a student at the Nature Awareness School I learned to pay attention to my dreams. And almost ten years after she passed, I had a very real and vivid dream with her. In the dream, I got to spend time talking with her. She looked wonderful. She was in her prime and had been swimming a lot for exercise. She was sewing and had made herself a skirt. We talked as she was creating more things and knitting. Over the course of the dream, we shared our love of paintings and discussed all sorts of topics. In a very real sense there was no limit on time in the dream. It felt like no time had gone by since she had left her body and it seemed like we talked for hours and hours, yet my entry in my dream journal was very short. How can a dynamic and real experience like this fit on a piece of paper?

This dream filled a small hole inside that felt like I had missed out on being able to really talk with her before she died. While we may forget from time to time what is dear to us, or forget the prayers in our hearts, the Divine does not forget and will lead us to opportunities or give us dreams to fulfill these prayers. While it was a simple dream, of just talking with my grandmother, it showed me how every whisper in our hearts is heard and is important to our Heavenly Father. We are so dearly loved, and so deeply known. Something important to us is important to Our Father as well. We have not been forgotten. And neither have our loved ones. They live on and can return in dreams to give us comfort or reassurance that all is well.

Written by Molly Comfort

21

One More Chance to Hug Mom

How much joy have they cost us - the things we wish we had done differently? Of all the things that can rob us of our peace, regret is near the top of the list. Fortunately, within the worlds of God it is never too late and anything is possible.

My mother suddenly became ill while I was in college. When I received the call that she had a heart attack and was in the hospital under going surgery, I stopped everything to make the long trip home to see her. It turned out that she would need lots of time and love to recover. We have a large family and everyone initially was helping out, but soon my siblings needed to return to their work and families. I decided to stay longer to help, knowing this was something I could do. I felt strongly that I both needed and wanted to be there with my mother. I had not lived at home for many years. That was an experience in itself, and also to be the one caring for her and my disabled sister. I was happy to be able to do it.

After my mother returned home from the hospital we were able to share time alone together. That had not happened for a long time and we were enjoying each other's company. We always had a good relationship, but I felt there was such a blessing given to us in that short time that strengthened our love connection. That time was a gift from God.

After several days my oldest sister planned to visit and spend some time with mom, which would give me a break. She got to my mom's house as I was getting ready to leave. I always had a loving relationship with my mom, but she wasn't necessarily physically affectionate. I wasn't either. My mom was sitting in her chair as I prepared to leave. I smiled, patted her on the head, and told her I would see her soon. She smiled and gave a little laugh.

I drove home for the weekend and I was barely in the door when the phone rang. My brother was calling to say that my mother had just passed away. I heard the words, but struggled to process them in that moment. I recognized later that was also a blessing. My lasting memory of my mother is the quality time we spent together in her final days. I was given some precious time with her, but spared being there when she passed. I have grown and know there is nothing to be afraid of and that God is with us, but at that point in my life I'm not sure how I would have handled it. I trust God's timing and am thankful for it.

However for quite a long time, years in fact, I would periodically think about that last moment with my mom. Why didn't I just hug her? I wanted to, but it was always an uncomfortable thing for me and I thought for her as well. I would tell myself I knew the love was there and that was fine. Then one day I was shown a different thought by the Divine. Why regret? Why not still do it? That day had gone, but I knew about spiritual traveling as Soul and I knew it was possible to see loved ones in Heaven. Maybe I would have another interaction sometime. That was comforting.

So I had a prayer in my heart to see my mom and to give her the hug that I longed for. That night I closed my eyes and sang HU before going to sleep. I'm not sure if the experience was then or in a dream, but that didn't matter because it was all so real. I was there. It was not in a dream at some later point like I thought could possibly happen, but I was right in that moment at that chair next to my mom on the day I was leaving her house. Instead of patting her head, I gave a true heart-felt hug expressing my love for her. And she hugged me back with so much love and gratitude. It was such an amazing and beautiful experience that I longed for and an answer to my prayer.

What a powerful and loving God that can hear my prayer and allow me that experience. That experience healed something I didn't know was broken. I am so grateful. God knows exactly what we need and blesses us through His Prophet.

Written by Michelle Hibshman

22

Family Reunion in Heaven
Part One

A family prays to send love and comfort, during a contemplation, to a loved one who has just passed away. They all three were blessed to witness her arrival in Heaven. Each having a slightly different perspective on the joyous reunion that followed.

Aunt Mildred was one of those delightful ladies who was always cheerful and a pleasure to talk with. I admired her strength and her attitude to be happy and enjoy life. Her husband and sister, who was my grandmother, passed away several years ago, and her health was failing. She stayed in an assisted living facility, but had recently gotten the flu and was very ill.

It was a Sunday afternoon when my sister-in-law called to tell us that Aunt Mildred had passed. My husband and our two children sat together and sang HU, asking the Prophet of the times to bless her during this time of transition. As I sang HU and was in contemplation I saw a beautiful field of green grass with rolling hills beyond. In the distance I saw a beautiful white city with tall white spires. In the field family and friends who were already in Heaven gathered with joy and excitement to welcome Aunt Mildred.

As she walked towards the group, her smile was huge and her eyes were bright with joy and wonder. As she came close to her deceased husband Chet, he stood still for a moment. He looked as though he had a lump in his throat; so overcome with emotion that he could not move or speak. Then he took a step towards her and she paused for a moment, tilted her head a bit as she looked at him sweetly, and then they embraced tightly, as though they would never let each other go. Grandma stood beside them in anticipation to welcome her sister. They embraced and then Aunt Mildred smiled broadly as she looked up to see the next person to welcome her. Grandma turned to me with eyes very bright and loving, and as I hugged her I must have said, "I love you Grandma," for she said to me, "I love you too dear" in her sweet loving voice. Those were the last words that we had said to each other just before she died several years earlier. It was as though we picked up right where we had left off!

One by one all of my family members in heaven came over to see me and I got to hug each one. Grandpa shook my hand vigorously, just like he did when I was a little girl. He was laughing and his eyes sparkled with merriment. My dad, who had died twenty-five years earlier, looked young and healthy as he smiled at me, taking in how I had grown up since we were last together. As I hugged my other grandpa he slipped a black olive into my hand. I was delighted to experience that again, since I had forgotten that he would do that for my brother and me at family dinners. I noticed that he looked much younger and appeared very healthy and vigorous. I realized that when we were all together on Earth, my family seldom hugged each other. Here in Heaven everyone was joyously embracing. Perhaps here they were freed from hang-ups and had learned something about expressing love. In Heaven there is much more to experience than playing harps on fluffy white clouds!

I prayed for the Prophet to bless the gathering and he appeared. Everyone turned to look at him and they gasped in awe. Being in his presence was a huge blessing and they knew that this was very special. After the Prophet left, no one spoke a word for a while, for they were so awed by being in his presence.

Later, I introduced my husband and children to their relatives whom they had not met in this lifetime. It was such a joyous, happy occasion, and it was beautiful to see Aunt Mildred with her loved ones again, and to see her healthy and happy. And then there was even another blessing, as our cat Tigger, who had died a few years earlier walked by. The whole experience was blessings upon blessings! Thank you Prophet for making this possible. It was a joy and a comfort for me to see them all happy and well, and to know that Aunt Mildred was OK and was welcomed into a new life.

Written by Diane Kempf

23

Family Reunion in Heaven
Part Two

From the moment I met my wife's Aunt Mildred and Grandma I felt a close connection. In my heart I loved them as if they were my own grandmothers. Both graced me with their beautiful loving smiles. I would see these smiles again in Heaven after their passing. I learned from my spiritual teacher, Del Hall, that Soul is eternal. Only the physical body is temporary. I was blessed to actually witness Soul's eternal nature following Aunt Mildred's passing. This priceless gift is still with me.

My first experience came on the day we received the sad news about Aunt Mildred. My wife, two children, and I shared favorite memories of her. We then sang HU, a love song to God. God's love answered and carried us to a Heaven where we celebrated a happy reunion of

Souls with members of my wife's family. We each received personalized gifts of love from God, with some overlap but each different in its own way. I saw both Aunt Mildred and Grandma with happy, beaming smiles. They were healthy younger versions of themselves. Both were meticulously dressed as if ready for church. Each radiated peaceful well-being. They were accompanied by a man I had never met before. When I later described him to my wife, the description resembled Grandma's husband. When as a family we later shared our experiences, we realized that the Souls we had met made up a family reunion. God had given comfort by lifting us into Heaven to give and receive love.

My second experience came at Aunt Mildred's burial service. At the gravesite my attention drifted from the pastor's words to loving thoughts of Aunt Mildred. I became aware of her presence in spirit as she stood next to the pastor. She smiled joyously, back-lit by golden light. This golden light of God blessed all who were present, whether or not we were aware of it. Aunt Mildred appeared younger and more vigorous. She stood arm-in-arm, reunited with a man she obviously loved very much. Aunt Mildred continuously turned to face the arc of loved ones around her coffin. She smiled lovingly at each person in turn. Without speaking she conveyed that she was happy to be out of her aged physical body. She seemed to rejoice that my family knew in our hearts, while still in our physical bodies, that Soul never dies. We need not live in fear of dying.

And yet another experience came in a dream. I was taken to a mansion where Aunt Mildred now lives. It is a beautiful high ceiling house of many rooms, a peaceful place of healing created by God's love. The staff members are very devoted to the Souls who reside there.

These experiences, loving gifts from God, brought me reassurance and comfort on many levels. I was shown the eternal nature of Soul as it lives beyond the limitations of the physical body, and that Soul is loved and cherished by God as it lives on in His Heavens. I have kept peace in my heart over the eventual physical death of my own body and others. This peace has sustained me through the passing of other loved ones, including family, friends, and pets. We will all live on as Soul. I am so grateful that God has blessed me and my family with this priceless gift.

Written by Irv Kempf

24

Family Reunion in Heaven Part Three

I was eleven years old when my great great Aunt Mildred passed away. She was in her late nineties at the time and it was expected, but I was still sad when she died. This was my first real experience with the death of a loved one and it was a little shocking. After my mom got the news that Aunt Mildred had died my family and I sang HU. We did a spiritual contemplation with the intent to say goodbye to her on the inner. During the contemplation I was not only blessed to see her, but I got to see other family members too!

After singing HU for quite awhile I was walking through a large garden. In the center of the garden were a white wrought iron table and chairs. Sitting at this table was Aunt Mildred and my great grandmother who had passed earlier.

She was Aunt Mildred's sister when I was a toddler. Also sitting at the table was my grandfather who died years before I was born. All of these family members were my mom's relatives. I walked up to the table and spoke to everyone. Aunt Mildred, my great grandma, and my grandfather all looked so vibrant, light, healthy, and happy. They were all sitting around chatting with each other as they did when they were incarnated together on the physical plane decades ago.

This experience showed me that I can still see my loved ones and send them love after they have passed. I also learned that our love connection does not die when the physical body dies. My grandfather died in the 1970's, great grandma died in 1988, and Aunt Mildred died in 1999. Now that they are together again in one of God's Heavens they still enjoy spending time together. The love between them was still strong.

Written by Michelle Kempf

25

Grateful for the Time
I Had

This story is about more than the loss of a beloved pet. It is about having the wisdom, trust, and strength to focus on the positive in a time of genuine sadness. Those who have this attitude of gratitude will be able to travel through the rough patches in life with less wear and tear on the heart.

I am eleven years old and I had an amazing, amiable boy cat named Adam. His personality was adorable and I loved him dearly. He knew how to give and receive love. On March 11, 2015 my family and I had to take him to the veterinarian and put him down. He had a urinary tract infection, which had damaged his kidneys. He was only three years old and I was extremely sad! I trusted God and knew in my heart this happened for a reason but it still hurt. Even so, I decided it would be better to be grateful for the time I had with him instead of being sad about the time I didn't.

I know you can visit loved ones in dreams so I asked the Prophet several times over the next few nights for a dream with Adam. I did not receive one right away but kept asking and never gave up. One night I had a wonderful dream with him, it was so clear. In the dream I was climbing the stairs to my room to go to sleep. When I opened the door Adam was sitting right there on the floor next to my bed. Once Adam saw me he quickly scrambled under the bed like some cats do. Sadly I got in bed, wishing he had not scurried away. He then peaked his head out with a look on his face that said "Oh... you want to pet me." He then snuggled up close to me purring loudly. I could feel his warmth as I scratched his furry little head. It felt so real! I cried both joyful and sad tears. I am very grateful that God and the Prophet knew I missed him. It helped me a lot seeing him again.

After a few months I started wondering about getting another kitten as a gift for my upcoming birthday. I then received a magazine I subscribe to and it had a kitten on the cover - which it never does. The month of the issue was my birthday month. I was then reading a book and the girl who had always wished for a kitten, received one for her birthday. I took these signs as confirmation of what was in my heart - I was ready for and desired another cat.

I will always have a strong love for Adam as well as for my new kitten, Milo. I'll always remember Adam and the amazing gift that God gave me.

Written by Zoe Hall

26

House Warming Visit

*Usually when we leave this world for the next we take
the form of the prime of our life. Full colored hair,
healthy looking skin and body, an all over physical
radiance. As if it is not joyful enough to be reunited
with our loved ones, seeing them in their prime and
knowing any physical problems they had while alive are
gone, is the icing on the cake. What a blessing!*

November 2, 2014 was the twenty-fifth
anniversary of my grandfather's passing. I was
only eight years old when he passed away. Since
he lived in Nevada and I lived in Virginia, I only
remember a few visits with him before he was
gone. But in the short time I had with him
physically he left an incredible impression in my
heart. His presence was one of strength, wisdom,
laughter, and most of all he radiated genuine
love.

His house was a wonderland for children, so
visiting was always a grand adventure. The
landscape out west was very different than

anything I had ever seen back east. He fit in with the terrain perfectly with his rugged but gentle demeanor, and he smelled like sweet musk, as any "cowboy" should. He was over six feet tall, which seemed literally larger than life to me and he wore western shirts with pretty snap buttons. I'm not sure if he considered himself a cowboy but to me he fulfilled that legendary role. His garage was full of tools to tinker with and a car collection I remember thinking must have taken time and dedication to acquire.

In the time since he has been gone I have been blessed with many spiritual experiences where I have been able to see him in dreams and during contemplations. One such dream was so vivid and brought with it so much love and reassurance. The dream occurred on November 2, the 25th anniversary of his passing, and I had been to my father's property that day to check on the future home site he had cleared for my family. My brother already lives on the property and it was very exciting to think of adding another house to the land. I said to my father that day, "I bet grandpa would be happy that we (all his grandchildren) are moving back home with you." My sister also has plans in the future to build on the land and I just knew in my heart that he would think it was awesome that his family was so close with one another, both physically and emotionally.

In the dream our home was completely built. The walls, doors, and stairwell were white and were just as the architect had drawn. There was a knock at the front door and my father and I went together to welcome the guest. We opened the door and my grandfather walked into the house. My grandfather looked about thirty-five years old and was beaming with excitement. He looked amazing; he was tall, tan, his eyes bright, his hair lush and dark, and even his forearm muscles looked strong and taut. I blurted out spontaneously, "Wow! You are definitely the source of the good looking genes in this family!" The air was full of electricity and we all hugged.

The dream was short but had a beautiful and strong impact on me. It felt like a family gathering, maybe Thanksgiving, when family from near and far come together. The love connection was palatable. My grandfather is a very pure Soul and has a high consciousness without even trying to. When I blurted out that he was where we got the "good looking" genes in our family I believe I was also referring to his inner beauty as such a refined and loving Soul. The dream was also a much needed gift of reassurance. Building a house is a large project and to be in the finished house in my dream gave me all the trust I need to know the project will one day be completed. I loved my grandfather's home when I was a kid and it was such a treat to welcome him into my future home.

Thank you God for such a wonderful grandfather and thank you for the blessing of dreams that allow you to shower your children with love.

Written by Catherine Hughes

27

Surprise Gift in Dad's Bible

The spiritual part of us, Soul, is eternal and continues on when this physical life comes to an end. Our love for others carries on beyond the end of this physical life as well. In the following story the author was not only blessed to see his father again, he actually received a gift in the physical from him.

My dad passed in 1994. I spent time with him in the hospital. Though he was not communicative, I hoped he knew I was there. Exhausted from traveling, I said goodnight and went to his house to sleep. He passed in the night. I knew it was going to happen and I knew Soul, his spiritual side, his true self, would live on. I was going to miss calling and talking to him and I was sad to see him go.

A few weeks later, I had a dream with him and my grandfather. My dad was healthy and happy. He excitedly said, "Look, I can walk through walls here," and proceeded to do so. My grandfather, who was seated, looked up at me and lifted his eyebrows. We both kind of rolled our eyes a bit. We didn't speak but we were glad to see each other, as we had been very close. I knew my dad would be OK and that my grandfather would help him in his transition to the other side.

About a year later, I came up a little short on paying bills. After trying everything I could think of, I let it go. It would be what it was. I saw my dad's Bible and decided to look through it to see if he had written in it or left a note. I missed him and was hoping to read something he had written. The exact amount of money I needed fell out of the Bible. I clearly heard my dad's voice saying, "I want you to have this." I was floored. In my spiritual eye I saw my dad, and behind him was the Prophet. I knew He had blessed my dad and I, making this possible from beyond the grave.

Written by Gary Caudle

28

Dreams of Dad

We live in a temporal world where everything has a beginning and an end. Fortunately Soul, the eternal us, carries on forever. This understanding can bring comfort to an aching heart. Even more so can a visit with our loved one replace our sadness with joy. To see them carrying on, usually in their prime, heals deeply and reinforces that our love is still, and always will be, alive.

I love my dad with all my heart. Throughout my lifetime I have always felt there was a special bond of love between us. My parents divorced when I was about twelve years old. After two years of living with my mom after their divorce, my two sisters and I lived with my dad. In the early 1970s it was rare to hear of a man having full custody of his three children. He took on that responsibility out of love for his daughters and wanting what was best for us. I have many fond memories of our taking vacations together as a family. We traveled by car to Florida, the Smoky

Mountains, and the beach. Along the way we made up silly songs and played games during our travel time together. Even as a young girl it touched my heart that he would work his full time day job as a teacher and then teach night school a couple of nights a week to meet the expenses of raising three teenage daughters.

One sweet memory I have is when I was about fifteen years old. Dad, my sisters, and I were "window shopping" at an outdoor shopping center. We came upon a shoe store that displayed its shoe selection behind glass windows. I saw a pair of red shoes that caught my eye. Dad could tell I really liked those shoes. I wanted them to wear at an upcoming school dance. He said he was sorry that he really couldn't afford to buy them. I felt a little disappointed but truly understood, and forgot about them. A few days later, dad called me into the living room and pointed to a box that he had put on the sofa. It had my name on it. I opened the box and there were the red shoes! Somehow he had found a way to purchase those red shoes for me, knowing how much I wanted them. My heart was so deeply touched by his gift of love. I cried tears of joy and gratitude, which made dad cry too.

I was so happy for him when he met, fell in love with, and married my step mom. I love her dearly. When I was a single woman for many years, dad and my step mom would help me with the upkeep of my house and yard work, and would "babysit" my Black Labrador Retriever when I was out of town. Dad was a loving, caring, and giving Soul. He had a delightful sense of humor. Of all the holidays he loved Christmas the most. He loved having the family over to his and my step mom's home for Christmas dinner together, and gathering together in the family room to open gifts. His trademark at Christmas was wearing one red sock and one green sock. Dad always said a prayer before meals and at Christmas he would thank God for the birth of His Son Jesus Christ, the true meaning of Christmas.

My dad passed away in 2005 at the age of seventy-eight. He started declining in health about a year before he passed, particularly the last couple of months. He lost a lot of weight and became unstable on his feet, struggling to stand and walk. He became depressed, started showing signs of dementia, and lost his will to live. It made me so very sad to see him in that condition. He had told my step mom that he was ready to die. The Wednesday before he died he woke up that morning and told my step mom that he was going to die that day. He said he had a talk with Jesus, whom he loved with all of his heart, and they had come to an agreement that it was time for dad to die and move on to be with Jesus in Heaven. Dad fell that evening and died two days later. In essence, he started dying that Wednesday when he fell.

He passed away on December 23, which was bittersweet because it was two days before his favorite holiday, Christmas Day. It was truly a blessing, an amazing gift of love from God that my family was quickly brought together in time to be with dad at his bedside when he died. He, as an eternal Soul, arose out of his declining failing body to Heaven, to loved ones who had passed before him and were waiting to greet and welcome him. A few months before dad died, my spiritual guide and teacher the Prophet helped me realize that dad and I had been together in several lifetimes, in loving relationships. That helped me better understand the special bond of love I had with him. After dad passed, even though I knew he was fine and much better off, my heart literally ached for a long time and I cried many tears. I missed him so much.

In the spring of 2007 I had a dream about my dad. He was joyfully dancing around with a big smile on his face, looking straight at me. He was kicking his feet upward one at a time as he danced around, and he was shedding / removing his old clothes and throwing them up in the air and celebrating! It brought me great joy and comfort to see him and know he really was fine, happy, and healthy. The Prophet helped me understand the dream, that it meant dad was "shedding his old body" in order to get a new healthy body on the plane in which he was now living.

Some time later I had another dream about dad. He was much younger, in his thirties, and looked like he was in the prime of health. He was outdoors either getting ready to get into an automobile or perhaps getting ready to work on one. He did that as a profession for many years – auto body repair work - and then taught auto body repair courses at a vocational school for twenty years. In that dream he was smiling his beautiful, familiar smile. To see him young and happy and healthy, and there was an automobile in the dream (which was so much a part of him) was comforting to me and really warmed my heart. This dream brought me great joy and peace. These dreams are gifts of love from my

Divine Father whom I love with all of my heart and to whom I am so deeply grateful. Reliving and re-experiencing these dreams continue to bless me with joy, comfort, warm memories, and the deep love I feel for my dad.

Written by Cathy Sandman

29

My Childhood Dog

Learning more about giving and receiving love is a huge part of why we are on Earth. For this endeavor - pets can be some of our greatest teachers. They afford us many opportunities to grow in love. What joy it is to see a beloved pet again after they have passed.

As a child I grew up with a very loving and excitable yellow Labrador Retriever named Izzy. She was not the smartest dog in the world, but she made up for it with a giant heart. Thinking back to my time with her puts a huge grin on my face and a tear of happiness in my eye.

She died abruptly of a heart attack almost ten years ago and I did not get to say goodbye to her before she left. I had been thinking about her quite a bit recently, remembering what a great dog she was. Without me even asking, God set up a huge gift for me. He must have known how much I wanted a few more moments with her.

I had a dream where I got to see her. She was so full of life and very happy. I got to interact with her, and pet her. I ran my hand along her back and felt all the little bumps and nuances that were unique to her. It was so real! God really gave me the gift of getting to spend real time with her, in spirit. Even though she physically died years ago, she still lives on as Soul on a different plane of existence. There she is alive and well. It was a huge gift from God to allow me to spend time as Soul with a pet that I loved so much.

Written by Sam Kempf

30

Comfort in a Scout Handshake

As any good Scout knows "always being prepared" is key. How though do you prepare for the loss of a loved one? Can anyone ever truly be ready for this separation - even if only temporary? I do not know, but having a solid understanding of the eternal nature of Soul can bring some comfort. Even more comforting is being blessed to see them again in a dream and know that it is real.

In the summer of 2000 my father passed away suddenly in an auto accident, which also injured my mother. My father left behind four grown sons, of which I am the oldest. He also had nine grandchildren who did not get to say goodbye. None of us had that last chance to say goodbye to dad while he was in the physical.

I had been attending retreats at the Nature Awareness School for a couple of years when my father passed. It was there that I learned how

God used dreams to bless, heal, give guidance, and teach. I learned how dreams were the trail head of a spiritual path leading home to God. I was trying to keep track of my dreams in a journal and beginning to realize what a great blessing dreams could be in my life.

A couple of days after the accident, while planning for the funeral, I had a dream where he and I met. He was clothed all in white and seemed to be surrounded by what I would describe as a Heavenly Host. There were many children present. At the time I assumed the children were there because my dad had been a pediatrician in life.

No words were spoken but he gave me a Scout handshake with the left hand, which spoke volumes, since he and I and my brothers were involved in Boy Scouts. It was a personalized gesture of comfort and reassurance. It was like he was telling me to "carry on - I am with you." I was able to share with family members, during our time of grief, that he wanted the family to continue with their lives and that he would be watching over us all. Many years later I am still grateful for that dream experience.

More recently I realized that in the chaos and turmoil of that week years ago that I had not been able to share the dream with all my nieces and nephews, many of whom were very young at the time. I took the time to recall and share it anew, as fresh as if it had been last night. In the retelling it seemed to trigger and give permission for some to reexamine their own dreams with reverence and anticipation.

We four brothers did not grow up with such a reverence for dreams. I was fortunate that my heart was primed to receive the gift of that dream by my teacher Del Hall, a true Prophet of God. That one dream has blessed me and my extended family over the years with the reassurance that our loved ones live on after death. And that it is possible, beyond the physical, to say thank you and express our love to loved ones.

The gratitude I feel for this connection through dreams continues to nourish and sustain me. It helps to keep my heart open for more teaching from the Divine.

Written by James Kinder

31

Mama's Kitchen

The comfort and healing from visiting a loved one in Heaven can sustain you moving forward in life. This love will remain. Knowing there will be a meal prepared with love waiting for him makes the author's heart sing.

My mother passed away one year before I had this dream and I missed her very much. This dream brought peace to my heart because I was able to see her and know that she is doing fine. I was so grateful to see her again.

In my dream I walked into a big new house. The house was simple but luxurious. When I grew up my family lived in a small simple modest home and seeing this new house was exciting. In the dream I walked into the house and saw my Aunt Lucybell. She greeted me with a large welcoming smile. She had passed away several years ago prior to my mother and seeing her again opened my heart. While growing up she was one of my favorite aunts, and I had many aunts and uncles. My Aunt Lucybell and her husband, Uncle Les, lived close to us and I could walk across a field to visit her and I often did. She would welcome me with a warm smile and she was always happy to see me. Aunt Lucybell would always offer me something to eat and I would gladly accept.

After Aunt Lucybell greeted me in this dream, I thought this new house was her house. The rooms were big, not too big, but just right. There were rooms for different functions; such as a TV room, living room, bedroom, bathroom, workroom, kitchen, and garage. I felt that this house was nice and I would like to live in it or own it, but I didn't know how I could pay for it. It had everything anyone could want in a house. In the dream I felt excited about the possibility of getting the house and wanted my wife to see it. I thought that she would also like it. I felt in some way that the house could be mine, but why? Did I deserve the house? Could I afford it? Was it something I needed?

I then went into the kitchen of this house and I saw my mother sitting there at the kitchen table. She smiled at me and my heart opened. I was so happy to see her! There were words said, but we exchanged how much we loved each other by the smiles on our faces. When I was growing up, the kitchen was my Mama's favorite place to be in our house. She would come home from work and start to cook. She would cook for us and cook for others, there was always an aroma coming from the kitchen of something delicious. Seeing her filled my heart with love and I felt at peace knowing that she was okay and also that she was in her favorite place where she could create delicious meals. The peace I felt seeing my mom was healing. I wanted to ask her about the house and if she knew anything about it. I started to ask her about the house and I woke up.

I was sad that the dream ended but I was also very grateful for the dream; it brought me peace and continues to bring me peace to this day. I can reflect back on the dream, see her smiling face, and the love we shared in that moment. It reminded me of the love we shared as a family when I was growing up. The dream also reminded me of the love that she would put in all the meals that she prepared. We had wonderful conversations in the kitchen while she cooked and I remember those amazing smells. My mouth waters just thinking about it! This dream was a blessing that helped heal my heart and I am so grateful for the dream.

Written by Golder O'Neill

32

Alzheimer's Loved Ones Get Second Chance

It is hard enough losing a loved one to Alzheimer's Disease. It is even harder having to live with any sort of regret for not being able to express your love one more time, or say you are sorry for something while they can still communicate. Fortunately, you can meet spiritually in a dream and have those conversations, even before they physically pass away.

One of the hardest things I have found about losing a loved one to Alzheimer's Disease is that you do not have a final opportunity to say everything you want to say, to make sure you really say "I love you" and "goodbye." You realize one day that while your father is still alive in a body, in many ways he is gone. You can not talk about your feelings, he can not share his – it's too late. It is a little like when a loved one dies suddenly and unexpectedly. I am so grateful to know that with a little effort, and by opening up your ideas of how communication between two Souls can happen, you can continue to have contact and all the blessings that come with it.

There came a point during my father's Alzheimer's that I knew we would never have a heart-to-heart in our physical bodies again; he was having such trouble understanding the simplest things, like where the kitchen sink was. But I knew that dreams are a very real place where we could talk. I let God know in prayer that I would like to clear up some old issues with my father before he passed away, and shortly after that I had a dream where we came together to talk. Ahead of time, I had thought he would apologize for his mistakes and that I would forgive him, but when we actually met in the dream we both came to the point quickly with a mutual, "Hey, I know I've done things to hurt you, I'm sorry for them, let's move on." In the dream I was my true self and could own up to my mistakes better than as my waking self. I got the sense that back and forth in various past lives both of us had hurt the other, but all that truly mattered was our deep love for one another. We were not going to count hurts and expect compensation, we were dropping it all. It was the briefest of dreams but I came away from it with a knowing that we had cleared the air in the deepest sense, and we could leave the past in the past and simply love each other.

After my father passed away, I discovered that my mother, widowed after fifty-five years of marriage, was not at all at peace about his death. First of all, she had deep doubt about whether there was life after death. She had a horrible pain, wondering if in dying he had ceased to exist at all. I felt honored to be the daughter she shared this with, and I tried to offer her my confidence that her husband still existed. That he is and always will be a unique child of God, not here but indeed somewhere, fully himself, whom she would see again someday. I felt some of it seep into her. While she needed to borrow my confidence, part of her trusted the reality of what I described. I left her to percolate on these things and develop her own confidence in them, knowing she should not be pushed.

A few weeks later I had the nudge to find out her current feelings about my father's death. I asked her if she had feelings of guilt, and she readily admitted that she did. She felt she had not been as good a wife as she could have been. At first I tried to reassure her that she need not feel guilty, that we all do our best but fall short of our own expectations. But then she said something that really struck me, "Do you think he knows I'm sorry? Is he aware?" This showed me that she had reached a place where she trusted he still existed after death, and this was a leap forward from where she was a few weeks before. Now she just needed to be reassured that he could still hear her. I did that, and took it a step further: "You can hear him too. Imagine what he would say back." And she did; she told me she pictured him reassuring her, gently urging with a bit of a chuckle, "Oh forget it! Don't worry about it!" I felt a shift, a release in her, a loosening of a burden. It was almost like he said it to her at that moment, as she described it to me.

Knowing we can work through problems with loved ones when physical communication is not possible is exciting and reassuring. We do not need to carry regret forever over words not spoken. Sit and close your eyes, sing HU, and have that conversation now. Or ask God to bring you together in a dream. It is real and it can heal both of you.

Written by Joan Clickner

33

My Diabetic Cat

Dreams are not just "mind junk" from your day or wishful thinking. They are a glimpse into the full life we lead as spiritual beings within the Heavenly realms. One of the things we can do in dreams is visit with loved ones, and pets certainly fit that bill, to continue in our love for each other.

Thirty-five years ago I had a cat named Tico. He came to me when he was a kitten, playing around my feet as I worked in the garden in the backyard. I did not know where he came from. The neighbors did not claim him, so I did. Or rather I should say, he claimed me! We shared a love that grew over fourteen years. During the stresses of my early career development Tico blessed me with unconditional love and empathy, no matter what I was going through.

In his later years Tico developed diabetes. He learned to come to me faithfully every morning for his insulin injection, which I lovingly administered under the skin on the scruff of his neck. The routine included a few precious moments of massaging his neck after the injection. I remember how he purred and cuddled as if to thank me for helping him in that way. His physical body eventually gave out, and Tico went to Heaven. I loved Tico. Tico loved me. What a wonderful gift from God he was!

Over the years since then I would occasionally think of him with fond memories. Recently I was blessed with a dream in which Tico came back to see me. He was young and healthy. As I held him in the dream and massaged the scruff of his neck, he purred and cuddled just like many years before. I awoke with tears of joy and gratitude. I am grateful to know Tico is well and happy and that the love between us lives on. I now even more appreciate Tico as the Divine gift he had been to me in my early stressful life. Thank you God for Tico and for this dream!

Written by Paul Sandman

34

A Conversation With My Grandma

Many who have lost a loved one would love a chance for another conversation with them. Beyond the conversation it is the exchange of love we seek. Dreams are one place these desires of our heart can manifest.

When my grandmother passed away I never had a chance to say goodbye. A few years before her passing she had returned with my grandfather to their native country of Switzerland to live out the remaining years of her lifetime. I retained a memory of saying goodbye to her at the conclusion of a family visit, as she sat on the terrace outside of her farmhouse, a spot that provided a magnificent view of Lake Geneva. At the time I did not know it would be the last time that I would see her in the flesh. As I was the youngest member of my family, and the only one who could not converse in French, I hadn't had much direct conversation with her during this visit. In her final years she preferred to talk with my family in French most of the time.

In the years that followed I would think of her on occasion, and how she had been a beautiful example of graceful living to me, as she had a calm, self-confident manner, at ease with her situation in life. She was born into a family that owned a beautiful country estate. She had been an excellent adult role model in my life as a kid, as she was not given to being argumentative or excessively concerned about politics, but rather was consistent in her teaching my brother and I good manners when we visited her. She was given to expressing love for things in her life, such as the church where she had married my grandfather, her pet dog, or the birds feeding outside her dining room window. I also remember how she had enjoyed teaching me a few basic expressions in French, just enough to get a feel for how it sounded.

It was almost thirty years since I had last seen her when the Prophet blessed me with a dream, one in which I was able to speak with her again. In the dream we were both sitting on separate rafts or small boats, on a calm peaceful lake, as we faced one another and enjoyed a conversation. She seemed as calm and relaxed as ever, as I asked her a question about a university in southwestern France, and may have expressed some interest in studying there. She confirmed that there is such a university in that region of the country. I then went on to say that I could learn French well enough to really communicate in it, if I applied myself fully to the task. I added that I was able to learn how to converse in Spanish in the past. I do not remember her exact response, but rather the feeling that she was happy to know that I was interested in learning her native tongue. She then gave me some instructions about how to get her dog, who was running around splashing water by the edge of the lake, to calm down, and the dream ended.

I woke up amazed by the gift of talking with my grandmother in a dream. It was so real to me and there was a sweetness to being able to have a true conversation with her. In the dream she looked younger than I remember her and quite healthy and at ease with being out on the water. When I shared this dream with my dad, he said that my grandmother had indeed lived in France, in an area southwest of Paris as a young lady, and that she had studied at a school during that time. This was a part of my grandmother's life that I had never known about, so hearing about it now from my dad made the dream conversation with my grandmother all the more real to me.

As I reflected on this dream, the Prophet helped me to see that the pearl of it was that the love between my grandmother and I is still there, as she is completely alive as an eternal Soul, at ease amid the spiritual water of God's love. Her giving me instructions about how to get her dog to calm down was in many respects an expression of her love for me. I saw the dog to be symbolic of my own mind, which needs to be kept on a tight leash in order for me to operate as Soul, and thus realize the abundant life that the Prophet leads us to. While the act of learning the language of the Divine has, at times, felt as difficult as learning to speak a foreign language such as French, I have learned that it is something that I can do. It is possible to become fluent in it if I am willing to discipline my mind, work at it, and accept help from the Divine. I truly appreciate that God loves me enough that through His agent, the Prophet, He blessed me with a dream in which I was able to have a real conversation with my grandmother. She is still alive as Soul, and still helping me to live a more graceful life, just as she did when I was a child.

Written by Roland Vonder Muhll

35

Together Again

You are Soul, an eternal spiritual being, and you will continue on forever. Your current physical life is like a drop of water in comparison to the vast ocean of your overall existence within the greater worlds of God. Even so, God can reunite you with loved ones time and time again. What a comfort it is to know we are not adrift.

My mother-in-law passed away from complications of Alzheimer's disease. Periodically I would wonder if she was doing well, and ask the inner side of the Prophet, Del, if she had met up with my father-in-law. He had also passed seven years before her. My mother-in-law never imagined life without my father-in-law. She missed him terribly until the Alzheimer's disease robbed her of even missing him. I knew from Del's teachings that my in-laws were fine. Yet I still wondered if they had met again where they were, or would they have to wait to be together in another lifetime here on the physical earth. I asked the Prophet if it was OK, would there be a way for me to know if they had met up on the other side?

In a dream about a year and a half later I saw both of them together and was able to talk with them. They were very happy and exuded well being. Best of all, my mother-in-law's eyes were bright and alert. She was neat and clean and not emaciated. Both were relaxed and peaceful. I have felt a lot of joy and peace receiving confirmation that my father-in-law and mother-in-law are together again, and enjoying each other's company. This dream also reassured me that my mother-in-law had been blessed to pass over to the other side before suffering any more.

My mom will be ninety-seven this year and is blessed to have her mental capacities. My dad passed away when my mom was seventy-nine. They had a long marriage with a very close love bond. I always believed that somehow they would meet again in another lifetime. Maybe my dad already had a new body? From my experiences and those of others at the Nature Awareness School, I knew that family members often come back in new physical bodies to spend another lifetime together. One day I asked my mom, "Do you ever see Dad in your dreams?" Did she ever! More in the last few years than ever before. Nightly, sometimes even if she lay down for a nap!

There were several recurring dreams that she had. In one they were in New York and couldn't quite come together. They were looking for each other, but couldn't quite meet. She found this dream very stressful because she so wanted to find him. She said that he looked so dashing in all the dreams too, in the prime of life in the dapper tall hat and overcoat that he wore when he went to work in New York City. It was at Lake Mahopac, New York where my mom and dad met when both were on vacation one summer staying with friends and family. It seemed to me that possibly this dream was prophetic, that my mom and dad might again meet one day in New York, with the same love for each other, but with new bodies. The timing just hadn't happened yet.

In another recurring dream there is a bridge with my mom on one end and my dad on the other. They meet in the middle of the bridge. I believe this means that my mom is still in her physical body on earth while my dad is in one of God's Heavens. They are able to meet frequently as their real selves, Soul, in dreams. I believe they meet often because at ninety-seven years old my mom is nearing her time to pass. I hope I was able to reassure my mom that these dreams were all real and good news. The dream experiences remind her that the love between them is still strong!

I feel very blessed that my mom and dad, and my husband's mom and dad had such a lasting and loving marriage. I feel very blessed to know that their relationships are far from over. One lifetime is a mere blink of the eye for God. When we have love bonds, and it's in our best interests, the Holy Spirit will arrange for us to be together again.

Written by Martha Stinson

36

River of Life

It is always special to see a loved one in a dream. When you visit a loved one who has already passed it is a very special blessing. These experiences can bring closure, peace, and joy! These are real experiences, not just wishful thinking on the part of your mind. The following is a beautiful example of this.

When I grew up I had a favorite uncle, Uncle Ed. A few years ago he was unexpectedly diagnosed with a life-threatening illness. He was healthy and relatively young, so this news took the whole family by surprise. Uncle Ed's health failed rapidly and within a year he was in hospice. Soon after entering hospice he passed away.

A little while after he passed, I was given the following dream. Uncle Ed, his wife Roslyn, and I were kayaking down the most beautiful river on a warm spring day. The water flowed gently, a breeze cooled our skin, and beautiful foliage dipped into the water's surface. The three of us enjoyed this day together, laughing and taking in the scenery.

We were each in our own kayak. At times we were close together and at other times we were farther apart as we floated down the beautiful river. I awoke with a feeling of joy and peace, grateful to have seen my uncle again. I know it was really him and we got to spend one more day together.

I know it was a Divine gift to see my uncle again, but there was even more to the dream. For me this dream carried another spiritual message. The river represented the "River of Life." Sometimes we were close together on the river. This represented the times in life when we were both incarnated and able to talk on the phone or be together physically. At other times in the dream, we were farther apart on the river. This represented the current time, when he had passed away and we were no longer able to be together physically. This dream showed me that even when we were farther apart on the "River of Life," he is fine. He is in another realm, but he is healthy, lively, and loved. I still miss him, but it is good to know that he is happy and enjoying his new life in one of the worlds of God.

This dream reinforced for me that our loved ones do carry on after they pass, and that our love connection with them transcends our physical connection. I am grateful for the teachings I have received from Del which made it possible for me to recognize and accept the divine blessing of this dream.

Written by David Hughes

37

My Mother's Love is Always With Me

The love between two Souls does not cease at the end of physical life. It is eternally alive and well. Not only is their love for us present in our daily lives, we can visit them spiritually in dreams and contemplations. What a comfort it is to know these truths through experience.

Each Christmas my mother would save one gift and place it on our dinner plates. I was always so excited to open this extra gift. It was one of the many ways she demonstrated her love for me. As a child I never thought I would lose my mother; I doubt any child ever thinks about losing a parent. I was twenty-one when she passed and it was devastating. I had no air to breathe; no blood to beat my heart. All ceased to exist. I had categorically never felt anything worse than the pain that accompanied losing my mother and I wasn't sure how to survive. I ached for just one more second with her, one more glimpse of her beautiful smile, one more hug, or to be able to say "I love you" just one more time. I would give anything to have just one more moment with her.

My father taught me from a young age to listen to my dreams for Divine guidance. I am so appreciative and grateful to him for teaching me the ways of God. Recently I was looking through some of my old, really old, dream journals. I came across a dream from 2001, three years after my mother passed. In the dream I was very sad and I was asking my mother to visit me every night. I was upset that I couldn't remember the times when she came to see me. She told me "I am with you every night, I am always with you." I asked her to please help me remember these visits together. I knew when I saw her in my dreams that she was indeed with me and I longed to be conscious of our precious moments together.

During a HU sing at the Nature Awareness School, fourteen years later, I was blessed by the Prophet to be united again with my mother. She looked so beautiful and joyful. The happiness I felt when I saw her is indescribable; I was overcome with joy and love. She told me again "I am with you every night, I am always with you." I was transported back to my dream experience from all those years ago and I knew that she has always been with me and will always be with me. She is not with me physically but a part of her is always with me. Her love is forever with me.

I cherish every time I am blessed by God to have another moment with my mother. I know these are real experiences and we are visiting with each other as Soul. These visits with her helped heal my heart and I believe heal her heart as well. Our love for each other endures, not bound by physical limitations. Like the gifts on my Christmas dinner plate, these extra moments with my mother are special gifts from God because of his deep love for me. I thank my father for teaching me the ways of God as a child; I thank God and the Prophet for blessing me with these treasured moments with my mother.

Written by Emily Allred

Epilogue

We hope these stories have inspired you with the possibility that you too can be reunited with your loved ones. Even more so, we hope these stories will inspire you to put pen to paper, pick up the phone, or better yet, visit with your loved ones now. Find time to express your love here and now in the physical while you still can. Life is short and love is precious. Do it now.

Love is not a matter of belief – it is a matter of demonstration.

The Nature Awareness School

The Nature Awareness School was established in 1990 by Del Hall and his wife Lynne. They continue to facilitate spiritual retreats at the school located in the Blue Ridge Mountains near Love, Virginia. Del is a graduate of the United States Naval Academy, and has a Master of Science Degree from the University of West Florida. He was a Navy Fighter Pilot and Jet Flight Instructor.

Although Del has a technical background his passion is in helping other Souls recognize their Divine Nature. Del has facilitated hundreds of spiritual retreats. During these retreats the Voice of God has responded in magnificent and life improving ways.

Del has learned to follow this spiritual guidance to the benefit of all who are open to personal growth. He teaches them how to have their own experiences with Spirit while fully conscious. Del then helps with the understanding and integrating of these experiences into daily life. Abundance follows.

Del's son joined the school as an instructor after fifteen years of in-class training to develop and lead the Dream Study Retreats. Del IV also lives on the school property in the beautiful Blue Ridge Mountains with his family. He is a nationally exhibited artist who attended the School of the Museum of Fine Arts in Boston and has paintings in over seventy-five public and private collections.

During the Dream Study Retreats Del IV teaches people about the rich history of dream study and how to better recall their own dreams. As an ancient source of wisdom, dreams are available for those who make the effort to pay attention.

The off-site events division of the Nature Awareness School, "Uplift With Dreams," hosts Dream Study Workshops, HU sings, and accepts public speaking invitations around the country.

540-377-6068
natureawarenessschool@gmail.com

Visit **NatureAwarenessSchool.com** or **UpliftWithDreams.com** for retreat descriptions and schedule.

Weekly Inspiration

Some of the stories in "Visit Loved Ones in Heaven" originally appeared on the Nature Awareness School's online publication "Weekly Inspiration." To sign up for email notifications of new posts please visit upliftwithdreams.wordpress.com

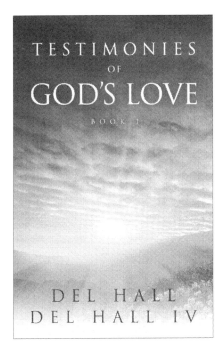

TESTIMONIES
OF
GOD'S LOVE

BOOK 1

DEL HALL
DEL HALL IV

What if God is actively trying to communicate with you in order to bless all areas of your life but you do not know God's special language? God is a living God. He sends His Prophets to teach the Language of the Divine and to show His children the way home to their Father. Divine love and guidance has always been and is still available to you. Learning how to listen, trust, and respond to this guidance will improve your life and bring more abundance to your heart. Within these pages are miraculous modern day testimonies written by students of the Nature Awareness School. Here they learned how to recognize God's guiding hand in all areas of their lives. Through dreams, Divine insight, experiencing the Light and sound of God directly, or traveling with an inner guide into the HEAVENS these true stories show us God is indeed alive and still communicating. These testimonies show how God is reaching out and desires to develop a more personal and loving relationship with each of us. These testimonies will shatter any limitations to what is truly possible in your relationship with God. They show how others are experiencing God's love and grace and will serve as inspiration on your own journey home to the Heart of God.

Made in the USA
San Bernardino, CA
12 June 2015